Immigration & Justice For Our Neighbors

edited by

Jennifer Clark and Miriam Downey

Justice
For Our
Neighbors
A United Methodist Immigration Ministry
West Michigan

Justice For Our Neighbors (JFON) is a ministry of hospitality that welcomes immigrants into our communities by providing affordable, high-quality immigration legal services, engaging in advocacy for immigrants' rights and offering education to communities of faith and the public. Founded in 1999 as a ministry within the United Methodist Committee on Relief (UMCOR), JFON provides immigration legal services to those earning 200% of poverty or less.

As part of this network of nationwide legal clinics, JFON-West Michigan began in 2004 with a site hosted at Grand Rapids First United Methodist Church. In 2005, it opened a second site in Holland. In 2015, two more satellite clinics opened, one in Traverse City and one in Kalamazoo. JFON depends on support from people like you for 100% of its operating funds.

To support the critical grassroots work being done in the Kalamazoo area, all proceeds from the anthology will go to Justice For Our Neighbors-Kalamazoo.

We thank all the writers and poets who embraced this project. You are as generous as you are talented.

Interested in joining your voice with theirs and supporting Justice For Our Neighbors-Kalamazoo? Write to:

Justice For Our Neighbors-Kalamazoo
212 S. Park
Kalamazoo, MI 49007

Or call JFON Kalamazoo at *(888) 718.7775* or email:
kzoo_assist@jfonwestmichigan.org.

More information about JFON can be found at *www.jfonwestmichigan.org* or at *www.njfon.org.*

This book is dedicated to the immigrants who come through the doors of JFON Kalamazoo and all JFON clinics, and to the inspired and faithful workers who seek to help them find a better life in Kalamazoo, in Michigan, and in the United States.

Table of Contents

1

5

They're Neighbors of Mine / *Scott Russell Sanders*

Loving one's neighbors, or at least caring for them without expecting to be paid, is in keeping with instructions from many of the world's scriptures, including the Bible, a respected authority in the community where I grew up. In that community, in that era, people looked after one another, trusting that they would be looked after in turn. They shared their abundance — of sweet corn, say, or plumbing skills — trusting that they would benefit from the abundance of others. Compassion might reinforce this mutual care, as when my mother hustled the shivering Thompson children into our house and fondly patted their heads, but the essential motive was practical. Being able to rely on neighbors made everyone more secure.

Anthropologists call this nonmonetary exchange of goods and aid "reciprocity," and they find it in every long-lasting culture. As a boy, I learned to call it neighborliness. Hearing that word today, one might be tempted to sigh or shudder — sigh, if one imagines that people have become too selfish, too plugged-in, too mercenary to care for others; shudder, if one fears that neighbors will pry into one's business or add to one's responsibilities.

Isn't life easier if we mind our own business and let others mind theirs? Isn't the American way to be self-reliant, pull yourself up by your bootstraps and let others fend for themselves? Besides, who counts as a neighbor? Is it simply the person next door, whose house might burn down? Is it anyone who lives on my block or my stretch of road? Should I consider as neighbors everyone in my town or city? All the members of my tribe, ethnic group or social class? All those who salute the same flag or worship the same god? Anybody anywhere who needs help? Who is my neighbor?

*

According to the *Gospel of Luke*, a wily lawyer asked that question of Jesus, who answered by telling a story: A man traveling from Jerusalem to Jericho was set upon by thieves, stripped of his clothes, severely beaten and left in a ditch to die. First one and then another religious official, seeing the man, a fellow Jew, passed by on the far side of the road. A third traveler came along, a Samaritan, a person who by the customs of that time and place should have shunned the injured man. Instead, he bound up the man's wounds, delivered him to an inn and cared for him through the night. Next morning, he paid the innkeeper the equivalent of two days' wages to look after the man until he, the Samaritan,

6

could return and pay whatever additional charges there might be. On finishing his story, Jesus asked the lawyer, "Which of these three, do you think, was a neighbor to the man who fell into the hands of the robbers?" "The one who showed him mercy," the lawyer replied. Then Jesus said to him, "Go and do likewise."

That was a tall order when Jesus delivered it 2,000 years ago, and it is an even taller order today. On a planet with more than 7 billion people, there are more robbers than ever, not only burglars and muggers but also identity thieves, online scammers and financiers who bundle bad mortgages and rig markets; there also are far more injured people abandoned in prisons or camps or slums. The media bring us news of ethnic and religious hostilities that make the ancient rift between Jews and Samaritans seem mild by comparison; they bring us news of wars, coups, droughts, floods, famines and epidemics. Worldwide at the end of 2014 there were 60 million refugees displaced by such turmoil, the largest number ever recorded by the United Nations, and more than half of them were children. Agencies ranging from Oxfam to the Pentagon have predicted that all of these threats will intensify under the combined impact of climate disruption and population growth, placing more and more people in jeopardy. Whose mercy can stretch to embrace so much need?

*

Psychologists first diagnosed "compassion fatigue" among nurses, mental health workers and others who care for trauma victims; in recent years they have observed the same condition among people who learn of trauma only through the media. Our screens blaze with images of disaster; our mailboxes and inboxes overflow with appeals for desperate causes. Dismayed by the scale of suffering, caregivers may burn out, viewers may tune out and all of us may retreat into numbness.

Yet neighborliness persists. In barrios, ghettoes, villages and leafy cul-de-sacs, along country roads and disputed borders, inside high-rises and apartment buildings, in churches and synagogues and mosques, the practice of mutual care still goes on. What form it takes will vary from place to place, from person to person, depending on resources and circumstances. For an elder in a slum, it might be telling stories to children, and for those children it might be carrying jugs of water from the public tap to shut-ins who can no longer carry their own. For refugees fleeing war or famine, it might be taking turns carrying those who are too weak to walk. For a teenage girl in a suburb, it might be staying

7

overnight with a woman down the street whose husband of 50 years recently died, and for that widow it might be teaching the girl how to bake bread. For a high school boy it might be sending a portion of his lawn-mowing earnings to UNICEF or CARE.

Even in a wired, crowded, money-driven world, neighborliness will survive. For we are a social species, with an inherited disposition for cooperation and sharing. We also have an instinct for selfishness, of course, a fact exploited by many advertisers and politicians and pundits. We are urged to think of ourselves as consumers rather than citizens. We are told that the pursuit of private greed will produce the greatest good. Despite these appeals to selfishness, however, all but the most affluent or arrogant of us realize that we need one another; we are responsible to one another for practical as well as moral reasons.

Anyone fortunate enough to live under a roof and eat regular meals might volunteer in a homeless shelter or community kitchen; anyone skilled in music or computers or languages might offer free lessons; anyone adept at reading and writing might tutor adult learners or kids who are struggling in school. Sharing money can certainly be an expression of neighborliness. After all, the Samaritan paid the innkeeper to provide lodging for the man set upon by thieves. However much or little we have to spare, we can donate money to support causes in our own communities, such as free medical clinics or after-school programs, and we can support international service organizations such as Doctors Without Borders, Habitat for Humanity or the Heifer Project. Even if we have no money to spare, we still have gifts to share — knowledge, perhaps, or laughter, a knack for listening or a kindly touch.

Before binding up the wounds of the man set upon by thieves, so the story goes, the Samaritan salved those wounds with oil. There was courage as well as kindness in that touch, for the injured man was not merely a stranger but a presumed enemy. Courage may or may not be required when we reach out to help others, but kindness always is. The Samaritan was moved by more than an expectation of reciprocity, for he could not hope to receive help in return. He was moved by compassion. To be a neighbor, the story teaches, is to show mercy.

The same lesson is taught in Judaism, Hinduism, Buddhism, Islam and most other spiritual traditions: We should treat with compassion those whom we encounter who are in need. We may encounter them in our travels, as the Samaritan did, or learn about them on television, or meet them in the street, or

8

find them knocking at our door. They may be wounded, hungry or sick; they may carry the smell of smoke in their clothes and need a house to replace the one that burned down; they may need only a shoulder to cry on or a consoling hug. That we cannot meet every need even in our own communities, let alone in the world, is no excuse for despair. If we feel overwhelmed by the barrage of bad news, then let us disengage from the media for a spell, look around, and see what good we might do.

What is a Neighbor? / *A group poem*
created by 4th & 5th grade Arcadia Elementary students

What makes a good neighbor is kindness.
If you are kind, it makes you a better person.
A neighbor is respectful, responsible, and awesome.
I want a neighbor who is honest and respects me
for who I am. They respect my feelings and opinions.
They care about me and my family.
A neighbor is a friend who keeps me safe and has a cat.

A neighbor brings me cookies and cake and cooks me
chicken noodle soup when I'm sick. I want a neighbor
who bakes me brownies every month for no reason.
Hopefully, my neighbor has kids my age so I can be friends
with them. I want a neighbor who plays with me and cares about me
and other people too, and loves us all for the way we are.
I can depend on them and they can depend on me.
I want to be a neighbor who encourages others.

A neighbor cares by making me feel better when I'm upset
and even when I'm not. A neighbor doesn't judge me.
A neighbor is someone to depend on when I need help
and someone to talk to if I'm lonely.
To be a better neighbor,
you must be a better friend.

I want a neighbor who is a good artist, plays basketball and football,
and likes to sleep. My neighbor helps me with my math and writing homework.
I want a neighbor who cares about me and stands up for others.
We could have dinner together. I would hope my neighbor
would care if I made a big accomplishment.
I want to be a good neighbor.
I want to be your friend.

**ear Baghdad, Iraq,**

You remind me of summers at the pool, the grill that made the garage look like a puff of cloud. I think of your sweet smell in the morning. Ohhh, how I miss you!

I remember when my dad got out of our small swimming pool in hot summers, and my sister and I would splash in the pool, and my aunt would come and take pictures of us. Oh, how I miss you!

Do you remember when my mom used to pick me up and drop me off in the preschool? How, in first grade, my grandpa would babysit my little sister and me? I really do miss you!

I loved when my friends came over to play and color, and chat, and have races. I wonder where they are and what they are doing right now. Missing my friends so dearly!

I miss it when we used to get all wet from washing the garage. But really, I miss you!

Thank you for being a great country, for teaching me, but mostly, for loving me! I will always love you.

Love,

Reem Ahmed

11

Here Together / *Lynn Pattison*

Because you cover yourself,
Because your food is strange and spicy,
Because I can't quite make out your words,
        I am afraid.
Because you move too close when we speak
Because of what I saw in old movies,
Because of what my grandparents taught me
        I feel angry.

Are you offended by my tank top and bare arms,
my sugary sodas and salty, packaged meats,
my loud and rapid speech?
Are you angered by what you saw in movies,
a certain *standoffishness* about me,
what your grandparents taught you?

If I share the comfort of a winter coat
        will you feel welcomed,

        If you teach me how to cook new dishes,
           will I grow confident,
If we learn each other's language
        will we relax together,

        If we hold hands
           will the space between us warm,
If our families go to the movies
        will we laugh in unison,

        If we meet each other's grandchildren
           will we feel more like family?

The Whole World in a Cup of Tea / *Kelly Zajac*

A local woman is taking a group of five Arabic-speaking men around town. She doesn't speak Arabic, and they don't speak English, so she carries a piece of paper where she jots down the English words for objects the men are encountering. She says the word loudly in English and the men say the equivalent of the word in Arabic; then they each try out the other's language. This whole exchange occurs during a time when Syrians are fleeing their country in droves as political refugees.

As this group enters my tea shop, they bring in an air of excitement and gentle friendliness. The guide tells me, in a softer voice than she uses with her group, that she is part of an organization that is helping these men get settled in their new country. Another customer who is nearby finishes sweetening her cup of tea, smiles wide, and says to the men, "Welcome," with a step backwards. I also welcome them into the store and offer them a cup of the tea I have brewed up and set out for sampling. There is some confusion and hesitation before one of the men takes a cup and timidly sips at it. His face lights up, and he exclaims, "Ah, chai!" to the other men. I watch as some of their shyness lifts like the steam off the cup of tea.

There is some exchange of language now between the two: "tea," "chai," "tea," chai," and people speaking both languages have another vocabulary word in their new language. A few more of the men take sips of the tea now that they know what it is, and in their sips I feel like they take some measure of comfort and we all set aside some of our previous formality.

I ask the guide to tell the men to return if they need other assistance, as some of my store's staff speak Arabic. I want them to know they have a place to come where the language barrier is removed, even if they just want to be able to get a cup of tea in their familiar language.

A few days later, a couple from Saudi Arabia comes into the store, looking to replicate the tea they know from home. He wears Western-style clothing and she is wearing a traditional hijab and abaya in the softest shade of grey. He is outgoing and social and she defers to her husband, which I have learned is common practice in their culture. They are not political refugees, but international students studying at Western Michigan University. They exude a warmth and friendliness just as the group of men did. This level of warmth I rarely experience with local residents.

13

The couple is looking for the kind of mint they use in their tea at home, but the man doesn't know the English word so he pulls out his phone to use an online translator. He types in the Arabic word, and the English equivalent comes up. Spearheaded mint, it says. The best I can come up with is spearmint, so I grab some for him to try. He holds it in his hand, smells it, and smiles. It's close, he says. We compare it to peppermint, and the spearmint is still closer to what he knows from home. I brew some up for him to try, and he and his wife sip the tea. It's close, but not quite the same. They leave without their mint, but with a stronger sense of connection to their host country, I hope.

Standing behind the tea counter, I have experienced similar scenes many times. We have visitors from England, Argentina, Brazil, Saudi Arabia, Iran, Iraq, Syria, Germany, Australia, China, Japan, and more, who all find familiarity and refuge in a cup of tea. Whether they are in town for work, for school, for travel, or because they escaped political unrest in their home countries, a simple cup of tea brings a touch of home and comfort.

I have bonded with a group of young Japanese women over sakura blossoms, Scottish women over shortbread, and Brazilian students over yerba mate. English women over clotted cream, Indian families over chai, and German men over rosehips. Each interaction is usually just a few minutes long, but has an instant depth that doesn't come with just any conversation.

As someone whose only international travel is from the United States to Canada, I relish these opportunities to meet and converse with travelers from other countries. It helps me learn about their homelands, their cultures, and their struggles.

A cup of tea is the thread that brings us together, adding one more strand to the invisible web that connects all humans. In all cultures, tea signifies togetherness and community, comfort and care. Through the act of sharing tea, I am less likely to speak too loudly or take an unconscious step backward when I meet someone from another country.

Welcoming someone into my culture, my country, is less about the broad strokes of public policy and governmental law, and more about sharing that which is the same in all of us. And what better way to connect than over a cup of tea?

Immigration / *Teresa Mei Chuc*

It is October, when the winds of Autumn blow strong in
the Pacific.

There are over two thousand of us, crammed sardines,
barely human and starving. We sleep on the floor and
wash ourselves with seawater. People are sick.

When someone dies from sickness, s/he is wrapped
in a blanket and tossed overboard during a Buddhist
chant.

I was only two years old and can not recollect the dying
next to me, nor can I recollect my constant coughing nor
could I recall seeing my mother's worried countenance as she
contemplated our future. How my constant crying made
her want to jump overboard.

15

My Road / *Kathy Rabbers*

I'm new here. I'll wave at the pickups
I didn't expect this dazed beauty
or this beauty to daze me
I can't get enough

Five years now, no hurry
I know I feel good driving by the farm
down the road, gray muzzled dog, horses out back,
how the farmer cares for his garden, bales his hay. I've talked to him
wife works at the hospital
the family, kids, grandkids string out across the country

He noticed I was driving a different car
I liked that
I am a part of his observances
like he is mine
like we could sit, not knowing each other
and talk for hours, I'll bet
I could count on him and he, me

My neighbor, such a place to fall into
this land, in my heart
Now I think he's rented goats
I can't wait to ask him.

Hands / *Jack Ridl*
   For my grandfather, second generation Bohemian immigrant

My grandfather grew up holding rags,
pounding his fist into the pocket
of a ball glove, gripping a plumb line
for his father who built what anyone
needed. At 16, wanting to work on
his own, he lied about his age
and for 49 years carried his lunch
to the assembly line where he stood
tightening bolts on air brake after
air brake along the monotonous belt.
Once I asked him how he did that
all those years. He said, "It was only
eight hours a day." Then he closed
his fists. Every night after dinner
and a Pilsner, he worked some more.
In the summer, he'd turn the clay,
grow tomatoes, turnips, peas
and potatoes behind borders
of bluebells and English daisies.
To keep away the deer and rabbits,
he surrounded it all with marigolds.
When the weather turned to frost
he went down to the basement
where until the seeds arrived in March,
he made perfect picture frames, each
glistening with layers of sweet shellac.
His hands were never bored. Even within
his last years, arthritis locked in every
knuckle, he sat in the kitchen carving
wooden houses you could set on a shelf,
each house a little bit different from the others.

Carlos Cardones: Workin', Workin' / *Elizabeth Kerlikowkse*

Workin' a shrimp boat in
Guatemala. Paycheck shrinks
as the boat rolls, dips.

Friends say you can walk,
walk across Mexico. No.
That is not possible

Family can't float
on that little check. I walk
scrub and chuckholes.

Workin', workin'
in Chicago, nowhere to
grow. Too much smoke. Steel.

I make mattresses
in Grand Rapids; I go to
school. The springs cut me.

I go to school, English
as a second language.
Learning is satisfying.

My wife and I hire
a lawyer in Nebraska.
We are citizens.

Kalamazoo? What
a name! New friends make
familia and comunidad.

After work we load the van
and peddle house to house.
Workin', always workin'.

Friends say it would be
easier to have a store.
"Buy a store, Carlos!"

We live on my pay
and save my wife's for the store.
She is a great cook.

Saturdays we sell
tamales at Farmer's Market,
gray skies but warm food.

Now we own a store
Tienda Guatemalteca
We stock everything.

But we are always
workin', workin' because
that is what we do.

Talking to Strangers / *Kathryn Almy*

Neighbors

Things I learned from Sesame Street and Mr. Rogers: That everyone is different and that's OK, and learning about other people is fun. That there is nothing strange about having Ernie and Bert and Maria and Luis and Gordon and Susan and Bob for neighbors. I also learned to count to twenty in Spanish.

Although I learned a bit more Spanish over the years, now, when I often encounter Spanish-speaking patrons in the library where I work, I am too rusty and shy to admit it. I am afraid to even say *si* or *gracias*, for fear of giving someone the wrong impression, so I leave it to my bilingual co-workers to chatter away.

Fortunately, Maria, who comes in each week to sell her tamales, speaks English, so I meekly order a dozen. (For *diez* dollars you can buy *doce* tamales stuffed with chicken or a beef mixture called picadillo.) I eat one on my break, peeling off the moist cornhusk to uncover the still-warm dough and filling. They are delicious.

Foods of the World

All the popular, storybook countries—England, Switzerland, Holland, Egypt—were already taken when it was my turn to choose a country to study for United Nations Day, so I picked Portugal because my grandparents had brought me dolls from a trip there. My costume was modeled on the fisherwoman's outfit: a plaid skirt, an oddly pouchy apron, a basket of fabric fish bobby-pinned to my head. On the big day, the whole fifth grade gathered in the gym with our parents to wear our costumes, share an international meal, and sing "It's a Small World After All."

The banquet featured many unfamiliar dishes—various dumplings, meats on skewers, plentiful pastries—alongside more ho-hum offerings like the Portuguese tomato rice my mother made from the *Time Life Foods of the World*. Seeking sweets, I was attracted to a platter of individually wrapped items. I removed the paper, which was printed in Spanish, and chomped down on what I took for a large tubular wafer filled with chocolate. It was my first tamale, and in an instant I learned how many ways you could be wrong about something based on appearance alone.

A World of Hope, a World of Fear

There is a scene in *The Great Escape* in which two British officers posing as Frenchmen are caught by a Gestapo officer who wishes them, "Good luck," just as they are about to get away. One of the heroes blows their cover when he automatically replies, "Thank you." My father remembered this while he was eating a tomato on a curb in Yerevan, Armenia, at the edge of an empty park whose trees had all been cut down for firewood, just after he had answered a voice behind him asking (in English), "What time is it?" But instead of mugging my father, the young man struck up a conversation to practice his English. They hit it off so well that eventually Samvel invited Dad to his home to have dinner with his family.

I have my own version of this story. While exploring the maze-like bazaar in Cairo, my traveling companions and I were approached by a man who introduced himself as Henny and invited us to his apartment for tea. I can't remember why we said yes (probably sheer naiveté, though I do recall a flicker of apprehension), or why Henny invited us in the first place. He probably wanted to sell us rugs, but he was no less generous when we didn't buy anything. We drank hibiscus tea from glass mugs, looked out over the souk from the roof of his building, and learned a few words of Arabic. And then Henny and his friend escorted us back to the spot where we first met, so we could find our own way back to our hotel.

Practicing

Four months before distrust of all foreigners began to take root in America's heart, back when travel was more adventure than ordeal, my husband and I visited his sister in Buenos Aires. We tried to brush up on our Spanish before the trip, but I felt awkward whenever it came time to use it, especially with my sister-in-law's friends, who were excited to practice their English and not at all self-conscious. I don't remember how we conversed, only the smiles and laughter, the feeling of warmth and light between us.

They invited us to their home in the suburbs for a traditional holiday cookout. The train took us out of the cosmopolitan capital, past ramshackle and heart-breaking slums, but Jorge and Susanna's neighborhood was neat and well cared-for. Their daughters showed us around the house and garden, and we played soccer with their dog, who, I was startled to realize, understood Spanish better than I did. We feasted on *asado,* various meats grilled in the outdoor brick oven. "Come back again!" they urged us when it was time to go.

One Word of Portuguese

While in South America, we visited the vast waterfalls at Iguazu, straddling the border between Brazil and Argentina. In our Brazilian hotel, I learned a single word of Portuguese: *obrigado*—thank you. *Obrigado* for the room key, *obrigado* for the wine, *obrigado* for the buffet breakfast and dinner, where every day we were confronted with an array of delicious, mysterious, and sometimes dubious dishes. Papaya did not taste as I expected.

Most of the foreign words I remember are types of food or greetings, but you can't go far wrong knowing *danke, merci, arigato, grazie, salamat. Chokran* for the Egyptian hospitality. *Shnorhakalatyun* for welcoming my father to Armenia. *Obrigado* for the *caipirinhas, gracias* for the savory *lomo,* the sweet *medialunes. Gracias* for the tamales, Maria.

Cross the Sea / *Naomi Shihab Nye*

A girl in Gaza

speaks into a table microphone:

Do you believe in infinity?

If so, what does it look like to you?

Not like a wall

Not like a soldier with a gun

Not like a ruined house

bombed out of being

Not like concrete wreckage

of a school's good hope

a clinic's best dream

In fact not like anything

imposed upon you and your family

thus far

in your precious 13 years.

My infinity would be

the never ending light

you deserve

every road opening up in front of you.

Soberly she nods her head.

    In our time   voices cross the sea

        easily

but sense is still difficult to come by.

  Next girl's question:

    Were you ever shy?

Woman with Child in the Souq / *Jim Daniels*

You stand, shrouded, bargaining down
the long row of male vendors selling black cloth
to cover you up more, and again, and always,
and I, the American Observer, see no difference
beyond the negotiated price.

*

In the hot street market bright colored birds
for sale prettily perish in cages. How many
words here for heat, for black? I have just one
and use each over and over.

*

Just one road leaks out from this city
to the moonscape, then ends in sandstorm,
ends without an empty Coke can or idle wrapper,
without signage or regret.

*

Brilliant hues, but still, their tiny hearts
blow out. And what about *your* cage,
I want to ask, but you are a black wall
I cannot lean against.

*

I have stopped looking
for street signs, addresses
or even an accurate map,
numbly circling roundabouts
among mad male drivers
hurrying to make a point
we have all forgotten.

They do not allow you
to drive. Even the sand
leaks sand, tiny irritants
endlessly defining survival.

*

Your son in his blind-white robes
stares at cages under blind-white sun
where he will be a prince. Or is already.
I cannot say what he desires,
beyond a colorful bird.

*

On scaffolding, imported construction
workers—how many words for invisible?—
insects fried by temperatures
that by decree never exceed 120°.

*

Would you take offense
at that, were we allowed to speak?
Me, an American Observer
with a superior thirst.

Oh, to be protected so—
what keeps your blue heart
from blowing out too?

*

He wants one bird, multiple birds.
They melt in his tiny hands.
Buy six, maybe one will live.

One day he will take a wife,
multiple wives. And what
number are you, and where do you
live? Where is your driver?

*

You can afford everything
on this narrow path of merchants.

A scribe will even compose a letter
for you. To whom could you write?

I am buying, what else, a rug.
I've been warned against taking
your picture. Perhaps we'd both squint
if our eyes met.

*

Above us, skyscrapers scrape, no magic
about it, tiny men up there who will
drop down to here in salt-caked sand-
colored overalls and disappear on buses
to camps out where the road ends.

*

The boy runs back
for you to give him something sweet—
sleight of hand from black robes.

I drip beneath the wide brim
of my American Observer dunce cap.
I pay full price for my opinions.

*

Natural gas creates all things
unnatural here. Out in the desert,
beginnings and endings blur with the wind.
Does either of us have any change left?

Oh, to be your scribe.

Blueberries / *Nicholas Baxter*

It was late, nearly 11:30 p.m., on a midsummer evening as I walked past the plasma donation center and a few bars, periodically staring up at the stars. Up ahead, I saw four people. Two large. Two small. They were dressed rather warmly for the evening and pulling along suitcases and carrying other assorted luggage. They halted under the corner streetlight. The two little ones were directed by the biggest one to sit on the short wall behind them and then the man looked around, then pulled out a phone.

"Is everything alright?" I asked.

"Excuse me," he said in concise English, "We are looking for hotel and my phone, is, not, working."

"What's the name of the hotel?" I asked, setting my to-go box from work down on the sidewalk and pulling my phone from my pocket.

"Holiday Motel," he said. "Thank you." Bathed in the dull riboflavin tinge of the streetlight, he proceeded to explain their situation as my phone slowly loaded the coordinates. A Ph.D. student with Western Michigan University, he, his wife and two daughters had been traveling for the past three and a half days. They had left their home in Isfara, Tajikistan by car, driving eight hours through the mountains to Dushanbe to catch their flight. From there, it was on to Almaty, Moscow, New York, then to Chicago where they boarded the last train to Kalamazoo. Some of their flights had been delayed, and they had arrived much later than expected in Kalamazoo. The apartment they had lined up was not open this late so, in transit, the man had booked a hotel. His family had barely slept. His wife said something, and he replied in a language I didn't know.

"Does your family understand what we are saying?" I asked.

"No, she asked what we say. Maybe they will learn English here. We speak Tajik. The little ones also know Russian from school," he said.

I was impressed by his clear and collected demeanor. The map to the hotel had come up on my phone a while back but I was captivated by these people and their journey of 80 hours across three continents and an ocean. They still had six miles to go to get to a crappy hotel, and then they would have to find their way to the university the next morning. How would they do it? What a terrible way to arrive in America.

"Your hotel is really far away." I paused and then, almost as a reflex I heard these words come out of my mouth, "Tell you what. I just moved into my home. It's three blocks from here. I have a pull-out bed and a couch. It will be tight but it will be warm, and I can stay at my neighbor's house." These people would not become strangers in my country.

The man wrinkled his brow. He turned to his wife and said something. She looked at me and I could tell she was assessing my character. I raised my hands to my heart. "It is safe and warm," I said slowly.

She said something to her husband and as they spoke, he gestured my way. As they continued to exchange words, I noticed the little girls staring up at me.

The smaller one with gold earrings had her hands in her lap. She had the same thick eyebrows that hovered over her mother's eyes, her face had the same solemn glow, dimmed with a touch of bewilderment. Her older sister wore brown bangs that framed her slim face. She said something to her sister, who nodded. I understood none of it, so I smiled. I didn't know where Tajikistan was but here was its future, staring back at me. These beautiful young people were global citizens, not able to speak my language yet, but saying with a gaze, "Who are you? Where are we?" Their futures would be complex.

My thoughts were interrupted when the man smiled and said, "She says thank you. We will come to your home."

*

I offered to take some luggage but the woman stacked a suitcase on top of hers, shook her head politely "no," and took the hand of her youngest daughter. The man did the same with the older child's belongings and I led the way.

As we walked, I explained how we were in the Stuart neighborhood, how it was the birth of the middle class here and how 100 years ago the road used to have a trolley. I asked the man about his home and why he chose

28

Kalamazoo. He explained he did technology work for a non-profit in his home town. He'd saved enough money to move to Kalamazoo to further a degree in educational technology.

He was lucky, he insisted. It wasn't often that citizens in his country could leave. When they did, it was almost never taken as a good thing. Liberal media, western systems of thought, and freedom of speech made it no easier to leave. Nonetheless, he had worked with so many other organizations and people that he had developed good command of the English language and was in a perfect position to leave. "It's about my family," he said tersely as we turned onto Woodward Avenue. "They need to be here as well, and I want to provide for them."

When we reached my house, I opened the door and helped carry the luggage up the flight of steps and into my room. It was empty except for two couches left by the previous tenants. I had some clothes in the closet but I didn't have a bed. Having been homeless just a few weeks before, I did not have the liberty of carrying many things.

I showed them the couch and pulled out the bed from the other one. The woman sat down on the couch while the man situated the luggage against the wall. The girls laid on the pullout bed. I went to the fridge and grabbed the Michigan blueberries I'd bought earlier that day. Offering blueberries seemed to be the most appropriate, welcoming Michigander thing to do.

Just then I remembered my roommates upstairs and, with a sudden "uh-oh" kind of revelation, cursed. How would I explain this? "Hey guys, I know it's midnight and all, but I just happened to encounter this family from Tajikistan stranded on the sidewalk. You don't mind if they crash here, right?"

"That sounds neither believable nor conceivable," I thought to myself. With a sigh, I set the blueberries down and walked up the stairs to explain.

*

"Like by Afghanistan?"

29

"Yeah kind of, I'm not sure where but they're just going to stay in my room. They will only eat my food and they will leave early in the morning. They might use the shower, too."

"Yeah man, I mean, they are here now," said John with a shrug.

I was elated! It was like finding $50,000 around the corner from a bank and when trying to return it, the bank doesn't know the owner and lets you have it. Except this was better. I had, at least for one night, a family of Tajiks.

As I walked back into the room, they all looked up at me. We all recognized right then, could feel it without words, that our lives had become serendipitously intertwined forever. Then, Ibrahim thanked me. He said it was like a gift from God and appreciated everything. I offered some blueberries, insisting that God works in mysterious ways. The girls ate some of the berries and their faces lit up. They said something to their dad.

"They love the treats," he smiled.

We spoke a bit more. I told Ibrahim I would be back at 7:00 in the morning to assist them with getting on the bus. He thanked me again and offered me some American money, but I refused.

"I will, however, take Tajik money, whatever it's called, if you have one." I explained that I collect currencies. He reached into his wallet and handed me two ten somoni bills, or $2.54 U.S.D. I went into the closet to grab the German Bible which held my collection and placed the bills in the pages between Titus and Timotheus. The mother said something to me in Tajik which I took as a thank you.

"You're welcome," I replied with a deep nod, my eyes closed.

I walked to the kitchen, grabbed two beers from the fridge, one for the neighbor lady and one for me. I had called her earlier, and she was so curious about the story, she couldn't decline my request for a couch. As I left, the mother was already tucking her daughters into bed.

*

The next morning, I arrived back home at 6:45 a.m. The family was already awake, packed and ready to go. I offered to make them breakfast but they

30

declined. Ibrahim wanted to make it to their apartment as soon as possible and get settled. They gathered their belongings and made their way out the door and down the steps.

It was a cool morning and the sun was just beginning to peek over the houses across the street. They followed me down Woodward and across Kalamazoo Avenue, walking close behind, their luggage clomping on the cracks as we strolled along. When we got to the bus stop, I gave them eight dollars and explained what to do on the bus.

I rode with them to the Kalamazoo Transit Center to ensure they transferred to the correct bus to campus. I explained where to get off and Ibrahim nodded. When the #16 Lovell bus pulled up, the family boarded the bus and waved good-bye.

I watched the bus leave. It stopped in front of the McDonalds on Rose Street, then turned right. As it neared the Park Trades Center, it disappeared from view. In a few seconds, it would pass the very corner we had met the night before. I wondered if the family would recognize the corner, if the little ones would turn to their father and mention it in Tajik. I wondered if I would see them again.

*

A few weeks later, Ibrahim, having messaged me on Facebook, invited me over for a traditional Tajik dinner with homemade bread, yogurt, and plov, a rice dish. His family, he said, was doing fine and loving America, though his wife was having a tough time with English. The older daughter was picking up the language quickly but the problem was getting her to stop when she got going. With her face scrunched, she gestured in search of a word for the name of the food they had eaten the evening they arrived in Kalamazoo.

"Blueberries," I said slowly.

The younger sister had been paying close attention. "Blueberries," she repeated, in perfect American English.

We enjoyed our meal. Afterwards, Ibrahim showed me maps of his home country. His mother had died recently. He showed me pictures of her and then of him, wearing a thick, black robe with intricate embroidery sweeping down both shoulders. It was, he explained, the traditional clothing worn to mourn the loss of a loved one. Her death had been incredibly hard on him, but America had raised his spirits and now he had a friend, a home and his family was safe.

*

In the Fall of 2015, I began my second year of service as a Volunteer in Service to America (VISTA) with Communities In Schools of Kalamazoo (CIS). As a VISTA, I helped CIS build capacity to meet students' needs and to support the college-going culture within the Kalamazoo Public Schools. On Tuesday, November 17th, one year to the day from the time that I am writing this, I walked into my new school site and was greeted by a diverse array of elementary students and staff.

I remember walking into the CIS office to meet my supervisor, Ms. Gulnar; a wise, warm, cordial Pakistani-American woman. She explained that she had once volunteered as a VISTA for America as well. In fact, she was one of the first VISTAs ever to volunteer for Communities In Schools of Kalamazoo and had watched our organization grow into what it is today. She invited me in to speak about my VISTA service, and we discussed my VISTA plans for the remaining school year.

After our conversation, I headed to the lunchroom to meet some of the students. I have found that this is the best way to learn names and faces. It allows me to gain kid wisdom, nourish my soul with their happiness and imagination, and, in turn, it allows them to become familiar with me and my slightly disheveled, bearded appearance.

When I entered the lunchroom, it was loud with so many different voices working at the same time. I walked over to a table and was about to introduce myself when I heard a shrill scream. I turned around and there sat Ibrahim's oldest daughter. She was pointing at me, her eyes wide open. Smiling a smile as big as the first night she tried Michigan blueberries, she bellowed across the lunchroom, "FRIEEEEEEND!"

We would spend the entire school year together.

$\mathcal{D}$ear Tajikistan,

You remind me of summer sitting on beach,
digging my toes in the warm sand.

I remember when my dad picked me up and
threw me in the water like I was a beach ball.

Do you remember when I cried when I felt a dog
licking my toes like I was a toy?

I loved when the smell of my mom's soup came
out of the window.

Sometimes I miss when my grandmother read
me night stories and put me to bed.

Thank you for making my life more colorful and
different. I am not afraid to tell people I am from
Tajikistan because I am different.

Roziya Rustamova

Roziya Rustamova
" Never give up "

33

Traveling at High Speeds / *John Rybicki*

Tonight my body takes
the shape of this city,
manhole covers rattling
over the pores of my skin.
I lean my car across
sparkled glass. Even in the dark,
schoolchildren race across gravel,
leap out at me, fingers locking
around the mesh of playground fences,
my windshield wipers
flapping them out of view.
As I near the house where my father was born,
the voices of immigrants blow in
from the suburbs, weave through
lots they've abandoned,
making high weeds bow down like wheat.
Near the expressway, I rumble over
old streetcar tracks,
pass the hard-hat crews.
Then down a highway ramp
that dips like a long gray slide,
feet first like a child.
Speed is what quiets me.

Crossing the Detroit River / *Bonnie Jo Campbell*

The manholes of Detroit steam all night,
windows break, streetlights burn out.
The approach to the bridge to Canada is a spiral
of orange road cones—you think you'll never leave.

From the river's edge in Windsor
you can see the Renaissance Center
is command and control. A lady fishes;
her arm is severed below the elbow—she got caught

in a machine. She used to be pretty, but
now she's too tired even to be curious
about the people mover. A Chinese man
is having a better day: dozens
of silver bass gasp for air in his bucket.

Shift Change / *Jim Daniels*

The Security Director advised me
to practice driving the hot mad streets
on Fridays—mosques full, streets empty,
city abandoned to silent heat.

Piece of cake—though I had not seen
cake rise in that flat sere land, vision
deflated by reflection and glare,
and I, American pork eater, unrobed
question mark of bone.

In my rented white Toyota designed
to deflect heat, attention, and Arab drivers,
I floated through wide roundabouts
of empty streets like a calm camel on holiday

until a sudden sandstorm of men
spilled from a gap between buildings,
weapons of prayer rugs tucked
under the arms of their robes,
swarming around the car as I sat,
unlikely rock in that determined river.

I flashed back to Detroit, shift change,
thousands pouring out factory gates
after their obligatory offerings to the lord
of labor—also Friday, also men.

Behind me, horns yowled as I scanned
my phone for a magic number. Nothing
to hold, so I held my ground— streaming
men in front, steaming cars behind.

Amid nameless roads and endless
calls to prayer, I was always lost.
An unbeliever in all lands, I sat
in hot din and turned up the air.

When I saw each man as one again—
human/space/human/space/human—
I finally drove on. Though I too
said an untranslatable prayer.

The Dump at Ciudad Juárez / *Alison Swan*

They did not leave home
and journey north to cross the tortured river
They left home because
they wanted to live

Now day and night the earth
on which they have built new walls
around their beds and chairs
family photos and statues of saints
shifts and shifts again

Of course their water makes them sick

Sleep lowers mothers into putrid gaps
that swallow children
Mothers dream of trees
holding their sons and daughters high above it all
In dreams babies change to birds

Mothers lay their kitchen tables with meals
and invite their neighbors in
They offer drinks of water
They receive drinks of water
They are planting gardens

Pathways form in the dirt
new house to new house to new house

Everyone stands upright
pressing crowns hard into the clouds
Mothers lift and lower their wings
and lift them again
Roots work their way
through the waste

Quan Âm on a Dragon / *Teresa Mei Chuc*

Mother shows me a lacquered painting on a plaque
of Quan Âm, bodhisattva of compassion, riding a dragon.

It is misty around the bodhisattva and the dragon.
The picture looks so real, almost like a photo.

A sacred vase in one hand and a willow branch
in the other to bless devotees with the divine nectar of life.

Mother says that she and other boat refugees saw Quan Âm as we were
fleeing Vietnam after the war in a freight boat with 2,450 refugees.

When she looked up towards Heaven, in the clouds, she saw
the bodhisattva in her white, flowing robe riding a dragon.

Mother says that the goddess was there to guide and save us
from the strong waves of the South China Sea. I should know

better than to believe her though she swears it's true.
I ask again and she nods, says really, I saw Quan Âm in the clouds

as we were escaping. I should know better than to believe her.
But, a part of me wants to believe in a bodhisattva, in compassion

riding on a mythical creature, to believe that somehow something
more than just our mere human selves wanted us to live.

Immigration as a State of Mind: Notes on a Poem / *Phillip Sterling*

First, the poem:

Neighbours

ul. Langiewicza, Lublin

Every Sunday morning the hot water pipes
that run upstairs begin to whine
before buckling down and filling the tub above.

Water flows for quite some time—the pipes
narrow, galvanized, not likely up to code—
quiets for the length of prayer, then arias

explode as from a German-made hi-fi:
tenors booming tragically some swollen,
scratchy song. The recording's never something

I can recognize (although I grant my operatic
knowledge to be small.) Other days I'm only
apt to hear her measured steps at meal times,

or a toddler's pitter-patter and ka-thunk
upon the unglued brown linoleum, an occasional
wooden wheeling of some child's riding toy.

I've seen them in the stairwell maybe twice.
She's thirty-something, I would guess—
a little pudgy, solemn, featureless. Both times

the child in her arms was so thickly swaddled
against the threat of cold
I couldn't tell if it was girl or boy.

Neighbours: The British (and consequently European) spelling of the title is
intentional. The poem takes place in Poland, where I spent a year teaching

American Literature and Culture as a Fulbright Scholar. Since my visiting professorship at Marie Curie-Sklodowskiej University (UMCS) was a full-time appointment, I was considered an immigrant and therefore had to register as such with the provincial government in Lublin. Beyond my students, who had acquired English either by attending secondary schools in England or Scotland (or, oddly, the Netherlands) or by having been taught by "foreign language" teachers trained in the Queen's grammar, very few Poles had more than a cursory understanding of English. But those who did, like the one or two residents of the apartment building where my children and I eventually lived, considered us *neighbours*.

Neighborhood connotes proximity, a geographically defined community, which some people acquire by choice, others by default. Neighborhoods are assumed to be internally dynamic. Whether or not one can be considered neighborly—that is, involves him/herself as a neighbor—depends in part on the nature of the individual, as well as the cultural nuances of the community. Immigration, in comparison, connotes a political separation—with status often determined by national boundaries and dictated by governmental policies (if not, in some instances, by ethnic or racial stereotyping and bigotry).

Neighbor is a term of inclusion; *immigrant* is a term of exclusion.

ul. Langiewicza: The epigraph to the poem refers to the address of the second of three apartments my children and I occupied during our year in Lublin. *Ulica* (abbreviated *ul.*) is the Polish word for street. We had managed only a few days in the first apartment assigned to us, which was university-owned and, by the administration's own admittance, "uninhabitable." Already scheduled for demolition, the grungy, one-room (and "sleeping area") apartment—which, we were told repeatedly, had served the prior (single) Fulbrighter more than adequately—was meant to be temporary, while renovations to the "new" faculty apartment were being completed. But "Poland being Poland"—as my department head explained—the projected completion date for the new digs had been pushed ahead, from "late August" (we arrived in September) to "maybe All Saints," to "the end of the year." Until then, the University had nothing else available, though if we were able to find more suitable housing on our own, the Polish-U.S. Fulbright Commission offered to help subsidize it.

The fact that we were Americans provided us with certain advantages while traveling through Europe—my colleagues at UMCS, a couple of whom had been to the U.S. as Fulbrighters themselves, referred to our passports as "golden"—but as immigrants, the search for long-term housing was a different story. Dorota, the young Polish woman assigned to us as a "shepherd" (that is, a translator and guide—a role tellingly defined today in the U.S. as "handler"), had a difficult time. Available housing in Lublin was rare and expensive. Most Polish families continued to share two- or three-room apartments clustered in massive, faceless Stalin-era housing developments—several generations together. (Living and sleeping rooms were indistinguishable in the room count; cooking areas and private baths were implicit, unless noted otherwise.) A family was considered well-off if the grandparents had a room of their own, the children one of theirs, and the parents the luxury (and privacy) of transforming the main living area into a bedroom at night.

Most of the apartments Dorota was able to locate for us, at an affordable cost, were either too small or an untimely commute away from the university. Or the owner didn't allow children. In one instance, when Dorota initially talked to a woman about renting to "an American professor," the woman was all-enthused and invited us right over. The apartment was half of her lovely house—the whole upper floor—and she offered to do the cooking and cleaning for me in addition. I could even have a small dog, if I wanted one. But when she found out I expected to have my two children stay with me as well—without their mother—she rescinded the whole deal.

We found the second apartment, a two-room flat on Langiewicza, by word of mouth. It was convenient, at least, only two blocks from the university, and while in poor order, the owner assured Dorota over the phone that she was willing to make upgrades and repairs as necessary, if we signed a year's lease, at 800 zloty a month, two months in advance. If only because there was nothing else, we agreed. But when we met to sign the lease—and our future landlady realized to whom she was renting (Dorota had learned not to say too much about us over the phone)—she claimed it had been a mistake. The lease was for 1300 zloty a month.

Whether the cost changed because we were Americans or because we were immigrants, I can't say.

The definition of *immigrant* carries with it a certain stereotype—often a derogatory one. As does *American*, in many parts of the world. Yet Americans who have not traveled extensively beyond the politically defined borders of the United States never consider those parallels. Years of fostering our country's self-identification as global leader, a First-Class nation, superior in many ways to the rest of the world (in market, no less than military strength) have bestowed upon Americans a revisionist history, in which we ignore how much of the population of North America is, in point of fact, immigrant.

Hot water pipes: I'm embellishing here, as hot water for tubs and sinks was provided by individual wall-mounted gas-fired heating units, which, while noisy, made more the sound of a propane torch than clanking pipes. The hot water pipes that the apartments did have in common were those of the radiators, a pre-Stalin-era building-wide boiler system that, at best, provided us on the third floor with an average temperature of maybe 50 degrees.

Not likely up to code: The speaker, of course, is applying his own class and/or country's standards to a foreign situation.

German-made hi-fi: The prefix *im*- is shared by *immigrant* and *import*. In 1992, Poland was still much in the throes of Russian influence, as it had been since the end of WWII, not only politically but commercially and economically. German, in this case would have been *East* German, a country of enough economic reparation and cooperation with its western half to be able to manufacture limited electronics. *Hi-fi* is meant to suggest a certain lack of investment in modernization—my father had purchased his fabulous new RCA stereo hi-fi back in the 1950s—a detail not only meant to qualify the status of Polish infrastructure in general but to suggest a level of affluence nonetheless. The fact that the music is opera is telling.

It is also telling—I hope—that the speaker, who seems to cast aspersions about the neighbor because she apparently takes a bath and listens to music instead of attending church ("Ninety-five percent of Polish people claim to be Catholic," my department chair told me, "yet maybe four percent are *practicing* Catholics . . ."), is the same person who admits his own cultural narrow-mindedness, his unfamiliarity with opera.

42

Unglued brown linoleum: The unfamiliar makes us uncomfortable. Immigrants are, in some respects, unfamiliar. Neighbors, on the other hand, are manifest in similarities, if only by association. The speaker in this poem has not likely ever been in the apartment above his; he's only guessing as to what he hears, based upon the time of day, or maybe what aromas drift down. In describing the brown linoleum, he's projecting, based upon what he knows—that the apartments are all of a single design, of the same age, and that *his* kitchen has a shabby loose piece of brown linoleum covering what was probably the original well-worn gray-tiled floor.

Pudgy, solemn, featureless: What he does know, for sure, may be a kind of projection as well. The speaker doesn't get out much; he's an apartment dweller of the worse kind—not very neighborly, even as he implies that it's the unfriendliness of the woman from the apartment above that's the problem. Immigrant or not, he's as much of a recluse and stranger as she is. There is no eye contact in the stairwell—that he mentions. Perhaps he's as featureless to her as she is to him.

Thickly swaddled / against the threat of cold: "Cold" is meant to be ambiguous here. We don't know if the poet is speaking about the weather or about the Polish mother's tendency to thwart illness by preventing exposure to germs. And it doesn't matter, really, because the point is the "threat," the danger of the unknown. That's what she is protecting her child from, which a perceptive reader would recognize as similar to the speaker's self-isolation, as evidenced by the details of his routine and domestic judgment, a metaphorical "swaddling," that is, of his own solitude and loneliness.

Couldn't tell if it was girl or boy: The fact that the speaker doesn't know the gender of his neighbor's child is not, as he is suggesting, the neighbor's doing. It's the speaker's as well. He has not made any more effort than she has. For that reason, the title is ironic. Neither the speaker nor his subject is very neighborly.

The current U.S. political and media attention to questions of citizens' rights and economic fairness tends to group immigrants as *them*, neighbors as *us*. A practice—if not a policy—of exclusivity, to be sure. Not unlike the speaker of the poem "Neighbours," who, it seems to me, sets himself apart by setting himself apart—making judgments and assumptions, instead of taking action, instead of making the effort that any "neighbor" would.

Untitled / *Lisa Stucky*

Brick tower of neighbors
Kingdom village
Emerging pilgrim
Journey not done
Reach out
Respond

ear Iraq,

You and I haven't seen each other in a while.
I remember taking the long way home from school just to stay outside
and breathe your air.
Do you remember when I used to sneak out of my house and play outside?
I loved your fresh air and delightful foods.
Sometimes, I wonder what it would be like if I could visit you again.
Thank you for all that you have done for me and for letting me step
on your ground.

Love,

Nabaa Eyddan

110° and Rising / *Jim Daniels*

In the empty exercise room
on the third floor, I'm elliptical —
luxury sweat in AC silence.

My car sits outside in its designated slot
under the sun shelter. Perhaps it will not
melt. Through the tinted wall of windows,
two small birds on the ledge watch
me go nowhere for sport, health,
and the American way.

I imagine them asking
what's your story, morning glory?
For I am the odd bird here, alone
in this room and country, signed on
to teach English to Arabs for a fee.

Even time evaporates in relentless heat
unworthy of discussion. My family sleeps
in the dark, far away, or maybe eats
lunch under sunny skies. I can't change
time. After a shower, perhaps
I will be free of sin, or reborn, naked
in this swaddled country.

How can birds stand it? Can I grow
wild, climb the fence, weave my way
home like a water-fed blossom? No.

Behind and above the birds, men crawl
scaffolding and control cranes,
shaping another arrow into the sky
for the sun to ignore.

Brought from Sri Lanka, Nepal, India,
the Philippines, thin dark men sweat out
their years as guests. If only they were
artificial, miraged, they could fly out

46

of my vision to their homes
where someone might recognize them.

My CDs spin, my feet skiing
through the antiseptic nowhere
to the dance rhythms of home.
I snap my fingers, cha-cha-cha.

The men will be bused to camps
in the desert, on the edge of the human,
to sleep where we will not see them.
We who enjoy life here. If it was as easy
as guilt, I'd be done with it at the music's fade,
at the squeak of the shower knob twisted off.

But when I emerge, a young man from Nepal
will bring me tea and cookies on a silver tray,
so happy to be inside
he will do anything.

Hear the Cry / *Mollie Clements*

Hear the cry
of the seven year old
whose papa is taken from him
as the family sits around the table
eating tamales his mama has made.
Two men in uniforms come.
They take his papa away
even though his mama cries, "No! No!"

Hear the cry
of the man whose wife leaves
because life becomes too much
    too hard
    too poor
    too unendingly miserable
    too disillusioning of dreams
even though the coyote
got them across the border
for their baby to be born here.
She left to spend her nights
    with multiple men
    who put dollars in her pocket.
He is left alone with his child
    whom he leaves with a neighbor
while he works too hard for too little
living in fear of the knock on the door,
his daughter left with no family.

Hear the cry
of the woman
whose husband is taken away—
deported to Columbia
to his village
where he is soon murdered.
Then she hears the knock on the door
and her son is taken away.
She gets the phone call:
    her nineteen-year-old
    had been killed
    by drug lords.
Hear her cry.

Family / *Teresa Mei Chuc*
after the war in Vietnam, boat refugees

When they woke up
in the morning,
all that was left
was the skeleton.

The bones of the father.
His flesh, not already
eaten by his wife
and children,
was stolen
and eaten during
the night
on the island.

On the day
he was dying,
he suggested
that his family
eat his body
to survive.

The flesh, dried up
in the strong sun of islands,
would be eaten like dried meat,
beef jerky.

A gift.

Not Just Another Conversation / *Buddy Hannah*

Sometimes you may get lucky enough to have the right conversation with the right person at the right time, and it opens your eyes and sometimes your heart to something that you have heard about but never really given too much thought simply because it didn't affect you directly. This was the case when I sat down to talk with Katrina Pradelski, a staff immigration attorney with Justice For Our Neighbors (JFON), an organization that works with immigrants here in Kalamazoo, Michigan, and throughout the country.

Not knowing anything about JFON, I did what any curious person would do these days. I sought the help of my old and dependable friend, Google. It's amazing the things you can find out just by asking Google, but that's another story for another time.

With the help of my friend Google, I found that JFON is a United Methodist Immigration Ministry of hospitality striving to make the communities where it works more welcoming to immigrants. They also provide affordable and, in most cases, free immigration legal services, along with being an advocate for immigrants' rights, while working to educate both the public and faith community.

Well, Google had given me some idea as to what JFON was, but it had done nothing in the way of opening my eyes or heart to the plight of immigrants entering this country. That would be done by Katrina. But I'm getting ahead of myself.

From the moment Katrina began talking about herself and her work with JFON, I could not only hear the sincerity in her voice, I could feel it. I have to tell you, I can deal with anyone who is sincere, and Katrina was sincere. I didn't know it at the time, but I had met the right person at the right time to have the right conversation.

We started out talking about her background, family, childhood, education, and much more in between. We also talked about how her desire not to be

50

poor any more led her to go to law school, with the hopes of becoming a corporate lawyer and making lots of money. It was a good plan and she was well on her way until, as she says, "God had a different plan" for her.

Being a devoted Christian woman, she followed God's plan. Katrina gave up the corporate lawyer idea and began to focus on a different kind of law, immigration law. With a new focus, she would soon be in a position to do what she would find to be her real passion, and that is helping the immigrant population. Also part of God's plan was her landing a job with JFON, which allows her to live out her passion every day.

By now, I was sold on Katrina Pradelski and her sincerity, but I had yet to understand the plight of the people she spends her days, and sometimes nights, helping—the immigrants themselves.

Like many of us, any information I get regarding the subject of immigration comes from reading the newspaper or watching the news. I don't personally know anyone who recently immigrated to this country, and I must say I still don't at the time of this writing. I never really had a meaningful conversation with anyone regarding the subject of immigration until I sat down to talk with Katrina.

From the start of our conversation, Katrina wanted to make two things clear to me. First, she wanted people to understand that, for the most part, the majority of immigrants entering our country are honest, hardworking people who are in search of a better life for themselves and their families. The majority come into this country legally, although you might think the opposite just by listening to the news reports. Again, another story for another time.

The second thing Katrina wanted to make clear was that she strongly believes there is no such thing as an illegal immigrant because immigrants are human beings and human beings are not illegal. Granted, the way some immigrants move and enter across our borders may not be perfectly legal, but human beings themselves are not illegal.

51

This is not to say that there isn't an illegal element involving immigrants entering our country. But Katrina and others like her, who work with immigrants every day, see a different element and that is the *people*. People who come to this country seeking better conditions which they hope will lead to a better life.

Katrina Pradelski and the many JFON staff and volunteers see what most of us don't see. They see the people who come to our country trying to escape the constant bombing of their cities and homes. They see the people who come here fleeing the constant threat of torture and death. The people who come here because there is no hope for them in their own country, and to them, America is their only hope. They see the people who come here seeking the freedoms America has to offer. Freedoms many of us take for granted.

In her day-to-day work, Katrina sees people who come to America for what they hope will be a better life than the one they may currently be living. She sees people who come to America to fulfill a dream, and that dream is obtaining a better life by becoming an American citizen. Even though it takes time and money to be allowed to stay and become a citizen, people immigrating to America believe their efforts are worth it and in the end, they will be rewarded with a brighter future for themselves and especially for their children. That is what the majority of immigrants coming to this country are seeking.

As an African American living in this country, I can make a strong case for me not knowing much about or understanding the plight of immigrants coming to this country. My ancestors did not immigrate to this country, and our plight as a people here in America has not always been pleasant, and there are still many issues today I feel we as African American people have to deal with. Again, that's another story for another time.

What I realize is, even with all the issues and problems many of us, especially people of color, are faced with in America, we still have the freedom to express our thoughts and opinions, a freedom many of the immigrants coming this country are seeking. We still have the right to practice the religion of our choosing. We still have the right to travel anywhere in the country without any restrictions, and the list could go on and on. In other words, with all the problems we are faced with in this country, our opportunities for a better life here is still greater than what many immigrants have in their own country.

Maybe a better life is what we should focus on when discussing immigration. Because no matter who we are, all of us would like the opportunity for a better life for ourselves and our children.

Now to be real with ourselves, we know there are people here in America struggling to obtain a better life for themselves and their families. We know there are people here in America who are faced with poverty and homelessness, hunger and despair. There are people in America who are discriminated against simply because of the color of their skin. We also know there are people here who face adversity every day of their waking lives. We can't and shouldn't deny this. This is an American problem. But to the many immigrants coming to America, these problems are not a deterrent.

Imagine, if you will, living in a war torn country and people dying by the thousands every day, or living under the dictatorship of a brutal ruler who has no conscience regarding the murder of his own people. Imagine being afraid to go to sleep at night for fear of being dragged from your home and tortured. For the most part, as Americans, we can't begin to imagine living like that. For the many immigrants coming to this country, whatever problems we have here in America are not problems enough to stop them from wanting to come to our country. Their thoughts are not focused on what's bad about America, their thoughts are on what's bad about their present conditions. People living under the above mentioned conditions and worse don't see the negative things they may face here in America. They see the possibility of a better life.

So I've said all of that to say this: How can we really fault anyone for wanting to come to America? I mean, come on, look around you. Wouldn't you want to come to America if you were faced with the horrific conditions that many immigrants are forced to live under? Wouldn't you want to come to a country where you felt life would be better for you and your family? Of course you would.

After having talked with Katrina, I could write an entire book about the subject of immigration. But I've learned two things about writing: every piece of writing, good or bad, always has an ending, and sometimes less is more. So, I want to end with this request.

I want you to first think about Katrina Pradelski and how she has dedicated her life to helping others reach their dreams in America. I want you to think about her passion and commitment. I want you to think about the day in and day out efforts she puts forth trying to help others find the better life they're seeking. I want you to think about the people whose lives she is able to possibly help change because of the work she is doing. I want you to think about the joy she experiences when a person or a family she is helping finally becomes a citizen of these United States of America.

Then I want you to think about having to leave the country you were born in, having to leave the only life you've ever known, having to leave behind family and friends, the people you love. Now think about having to come to a country where there is no one who knows you and you know no one. I want you to think about coming to a country where the only thing you have is the clothes on your back and a dream of a better life.

I want you to think about how that must feel. How alone you would feel. I want you to think about being in this country and having people treat you badly when all you're seeking is a better life for you and your family. I want you to think about this: what if it was you instead of them?

Now I'm not expecting that after reading this you will go out looking for an immigrant family to help. I don't even expect some of you to change your views on immigration. The best I can hope for is that you will at least think differently about the plight of immigrants and the dream they have for a better life.

And, if by chance you encounter a person in your community who has immigrated to this country, perhaps you will not fault them for seeking a better life for themselves and their family.

You will not automatically think they are here to take your job, or they are terrorists. You won't just assume that they came here illegally. And if, like me, you happen to have the right conversation with the right person at the right time, you might get a better understanding of the plight of immigrants and their dreams of a better life. You might even roll out the welcome mat for them.

ear Syria,

You are beautiful in my eyes.
I remember living together under one home.
Do you remember when we walked on your crust?
I love your gardens.
Sometimes, I wonder, "Where are my friends?"
Thank you for my memories.

Love you,

Nour Abdullah

After the Embargo / *Jack Ridl*

Let the embargo go. Let
in. Let out. Make sure to send
the cigars. We must have

the cigars. And another
baseball player or two
or three. And Cuban

sandwiches. The music
has been here for
a thousand years. It

needed no heartbreaking
raft to land on the sand.
It came the way music

always does. And now
along the shores of the
Florida Keys, maybe

one day there will no longer
be a sea-soaked, ragged salt
enameled soul dragged

to jail to wait, and to wait.

ear Syria,

You are a beautiful country.
I remember my school.
Do you remember my friends?
I loved to play at my house.
Sometimes, I miss my house.
Thank you for being my country.

Love,

Abdullah Tayara

I'm stealing a clutch of stones / *Marion Boyer*

from this English beach. They're flint, blue and white
as a mackerel sky. Here, in Norfolk, medieval walls

and churches are built with this stone. Today, the wind
blows strong. Black-headed gulls wheel and turn.

The North Sea hushes in as though soothing
a baby at the shoulder. Not far from where I stand

is the mansion where my grandmother was a servant.
As an infant she'd been turned over by her mother

to be raised a foundling and trained for service.
Everything about that decision, and the years following,

was hard, shameful, and never known in my family.
But I discovered her story. So I've flown to England

to step inside that mansion, to gather these stones,
to sit where she might have written letters over nine years

that sailed off to Ontario into the hands of her young man
until, a morning in 1919, one year after Armistice,

after all the dead, the bombed and gassed, the influenza
that shivered a body at breakfast then choked it blue

by sundown, my grandmother packed a bag. Norfolk flint
shatters like glass or it can spark a fire. Alone, she left

England and no one behind. By train to London, then on
to Liverpool. Three days in a cheap boarding house.

Thieves, mush-mouthed drunks. Weary lines at Emigration.
Children whose belly buttons nearly rubbed their backbones.

She crowded down the gangway into the *Saxonia's* steerage.
A narrow bunk. Constant racket. Oily air. Filth.

The wilderness of a winter crossing. Retching. No privacy,
leering eyes. Flint is a most durable stone.

Halifax, at last, in late December. What could she have carried?
By train to Toronto, then on to Windsor. And I think of her

finally, trudging to his door, unprepared for snow,
for all that might follow her knock.

Schwarzwälder Kirschtorte / *Bryan R. Monte*

I know it's bad news when the young hospital intern
shuts her office door and switches off her pager
her tensed face and pinched eyes betraying
a forced smile and good test results
minutes before she gets to what's wrong,
this time, with my brain, heart or lungs.

Which finally makes me stop thinking
about the Schwarzwälder Kirschtorte revolving
downstairs on the café's, mirrored cake carousel,
a gustatory miracle of cherry liqueur,
twin layers of chocolate cake and whipped cream,
as I pay more attention and time slows down
and she explains slowly, in Dutch, which part of me
they can't reach or cure this time:
another burnt fuse in my brain that muddies
even my English pronunciation, heart valves that
won't close completely, or a spot on my lungs,
acquired after a bout with double pneumonia
last summer, that now makes my laugh whistle.

I think of that cake and then of my gym-fit friends
thirty years ago, their tanned, muscled bodies
melted down in months to jaundiced skeletons
connected to tubes disappearing into more holes
than God ever gave them
trying to hang on a week, a month longer
for a new drug that would give them
weeks or months more to gasp, choke and sweat
and of the vacation days I had to take
to attend their funerals,
so many funerals in so few years,
I put a continent and an ocean
between myself and that place.

I think of those young men and come back to the room,
try to comfort the young doctor who hasn't lost (m)any yet,
tell her I understand my "options," thank her for her time,
and go downstairs to eat a piece of that cake.

Where I Belong / *Ritika Verma*

I am from hot sun,
    and cool breeze.
I am from nice people,
    and friends to meet.
I am from animals,
    big and small.
I am from creatures,
    tiny and tall.
I am from shops,
    where many kids cross.
I am from there,
    and that's why I shared.

Ridl Was Once Spelled Hridl / *Jack Ridl*

Bohemian draft runs
from the barrels of Pilzen

to the gnarled streets
of Prague where

Nazis spit
then rolled over

anything left behind.
Here my father

cleared the rubble
and searched

for something
to take home.

Today puppets—
tramps, fiddlers,

clowns, and ballerinas—
dangle and dance

their way along
the ancient stone

bridge carrying
each gray day into

the lingering song of sparrows.

The Bullfrog / *Hedy Habra*

Like a Mandarin,
staring at his silky reflection,
a Narcissus frog
seated on an Arrowhead leaf
thinks he is a yellow flower.
I watch him,
my own split image,
schizophrenic frog,
conscious of the Other in himself.

Teranga / *Carrie Knowlton*

You can fall in love with a person, but you can also fall in love with moments in time; the sounds of drums on the beach, and roosters crowing while women pound millet at dawn. You can fall in love with the way the Atlantic Ocean smells at sunset and the way all those things come together to become your memory of a place. After two and a half years living in Senegal while serving in the Peace Corps, I was smitten.

Senegal is that bump that juts out into the Atlantic Ocean just below the Sahara desert on the western-most tip of Africa. There is a beach in the capital, Dakar, where you can sit and eat a plate of fish and rice, watch the sunset, and listen to drumming and the call to prayer. The country is 92% Muslim and French is the official language, but there are more than thirty local languages spoken throughout the country. While serving in the Peace Corps, I lived in a tiny village called Niaoulen-Tanou where I learned Pulaar, a traditionally nomadic language spoken all over West Africa. I loved Niaoulen, but it was hard. I craved electricity and plumbing, cheese and raspberries, and feeling cold once in a while. I hadn't left the continent in over two years and was eager to go home, but was planning to spend some time in Morocco and Europe on the way.

I was excited about this, however, when I told my Senegalese friends and host family about my plans, they thought I was crazy. To a Senegalese person, being alone and away from your family is unthinkable. In Senegal, there is a concept called "teranga," which means when you meet a stranger you treat them like family. You feed and take care of them until it is time for them to go on the road again. Teranga can be loosely translated as hospitality, but it means so much more than that; teranga is a basic foundation of Senegalese culture. So, when I told my friend, Hamidou, about my plans, he thought it sounded like a terrible idea but told me that if I got lonely and I missed Senegal and needed some teranga, I could call his brother, Soori, in Madrid. Hamidou's mother got very excited about this and asked me if she could send a small gift for Soori. Very small. Just a *cadeau tosooko*, the tiniest of gifts. I reluctantly agreed.

On my last day in my village, we had a huge party, and I cried and cried. Women danced and brought me peanut butter, meat, yogurt, and many, many chickens. I turned them all down, explaining that I couldn't fit these items in my backpack and take them on an airplane. Then Hamidou's mom came with her *cadeau tosooko*, which turned out to be a giant plastic bag filled with 20 pounds of lacciri. Lacciri is millet that has been pounded by hand, dried in the sun, and rolled into little balls, kind of like couscous. She must have seen the horrified look on my face because she quickly explained that Soori couldn't get good lacciri in Spain. It wouldn't be that heavy, and she was sure her son would cook some for me; I would be so happy to eat it after carrying it so far. I wanted to say no, but she and her family had shown me so much teranga and she was so persistent. I gave in, although we negotiated that I would take only half of it, which was still ten pounds of millet I would be carrying in my backpack for the next three weeks until I got to Madrid.

I said goodbye and went to Morocco with some friends and after parting ways with them, I took a ferry by myself from Algiers to Spain. When I arrived, I was utterly and completely alone. I thought I was going to arrive in Madrid and take a hot shower, eat tapas and drink wine, and have a romance with some Austrian mountain man. Instead, I got on an escalator for the first time in two years, became overwhelmed by the variety of hams, cheeses, and wines available on the menu, and locked myself in the hotel room for 24 hours. My Senegalese friends were right. I was very much in need of teranga. I took a hot shower and called Soori. He was a poor immigrant who lived in a crowded apartment, and he turned out to be very difficult to reach. This was in the days before cell phones and each time I called, one of his many roommates told me that Soori would call me back. He never did.

After 36 hours, spent mostly in the hotel room, it was time to say *adios* to Spain.

I gathered my belongings, which still included ten pounds of dried millet. I took the lacciri out of my backpack and thought about throwing it away, but I just couldn't do it. It was the one thing that kept me still firmly connected to the land of teranga. I was on my way to London to visit a friend—maybe I would try to cook it for her. I put it back in my pack and left for the train station.

After a long night on the train, I arrived in Paris and felt a little more at home. My French is terrible, but after two years in West Africa, it was more familiar to me than Spanish. It was 2001, one year before the Euro, and I had about $20 worth of pesetas and some traveler's cheques. With one hour to spare before my train to London departed at 8 a.m., I thought I could buy a croissant and a café au lait. I looked around for somewhere to change money into francs, but all the Bureaus de Change were closed. My stomach was growling, but I decided I could wait to eat until London. I looked around for my train but didn't see "London" on the boards. I dug out my Eurostar ticket and showed it to a nice-looking French woman.

"Ou est le Eurostar?" I asked. She looked at me with pity and pointed at the ticket where it said, "Gare du Nord." We are at the Gare de Lyon, she explained. The Gare du Nord is five kilometers away.

I was at an entirely different train station. I had no map, no money, and a backpack full of dry millet. And the planning ahead that I had previously been so proud of was about to be wasted because I was going to miss my train. I started missing Senegal even more, because in Senegal there are no schedules. You just go to the station and wait until someone is ready to take you somewhere, and then you go. It isn't efficient, but it is certainly simpler.

I left the station to see if I could walk. I asked a couple of people in my terrible French where the Gare du Nord was but they pointed in opposite directions. I tried to explain that I was lost, had only pesetas and needed a taxi and was about to miss my train. The French people, with little patience for my terrible command of their language were politely but quickly on their way. I wandered around, looking for a bank, and then, suddenly, I spotted a tall African woman, with her hair in tight, expertly woven braids. She wore an indigo batik and a long, tightly wrapped skirt. She had to be Senegalese. To confirm my belief I went up and asked, "Vous etes d'ou?"

She looked at me with the weary expression of someone who has humored too many people thinking that Africa is a country instead of a gigantic, diverse continent. "Je suis Africain," she said. I took this for code: "I'm not going to get into this with you right now."

"Qu'elle pays, Senegal?" I persisted.

Her face softened a bit. "Oui."

"A nani Pulaar?" I ventured, hoping she spoke a language that I could actually communicate in besides French.

Her eyes widened. "Eey, ko mi Pulo," she replied. Yes, I am Pulaar. So I explained my predicament. She told me her name was Aissatou, and she had lived in France for four years and hated it. She cleaned houses for a living and missed Senegal terribly. She had never met a *toubab*, or white person, who spoke Pulaar, and had definitely never met a white person who seemed more lost in Paris than she ever did.

Aissatou grabbed me by the hand and took me to four different Lebanese groceries, negotiating the way she would at a market in Dakar to find someone who would change my pesetas into francs. It came at a price. My $20 of pesetas turned into $10 of francs, which she did not think would get me to the Gare du Nord. It was almost 7:30 a.m. and time was running out. She offered to give me the extra money. I refused, but she insisted.

Standing on a street corner in Paris, I suddenly remembered I had ten pounds of lacciri in my bag. I pulled it out and gave it to Aissatou. When she opened up her thank you gift, she laughed so hard that she was crying. I was laughing too, because it was the most ridiculously perfect thing that could have happened to either of us. Parisians were turning around to look at what this disheveled American girl and perfectly coiffed Senegalese woman could be laughing about in the streets of Paris in the early morning hours. I took Aissatou's money and address so I could pay her back. Because she is full of teranga, Aissatou insisted on waiting with me for a taxi.

The taxis kept passing us by.

Aissatou quietly informed me that she thought I would get a taxi more quickly if we weren't standing together. She stepped back a bit and a taxi instantly pulled over. We hugged. I thanked her and we laughed again about the lacciri. The taxi driver looked confused.

I caught my train to London and slowly readjusted to life in the developed world. Aissatou and I even exchanged a few postcards. I repaid her, and she invited me over for lacciri the next time I was in Paris. I have since lost touch with her, but I still think often of the teranga she showed me, even in a land where she was a stranger herself. I can never truly repay her hospitality, but in this time of mistrust for immigrants, refugees, and Islam, I try to channel her teranga and extend it to weary travelers I meet in this country, as well.

**ear Saudi Arabia,**

You are a wonderful country.
I remember my good friend.
Do you remember me?
I'd love to see my cousins.
Sometimes, I miss my school.
Thank you for letting me live there.

Sincerely,

Faris Bukhader

The Conditioning of Air / *Jim Daniels*

The grimy Guest Worker in line
at the hypermarket

is buying a precooked chicken
and a bottle of water. He takes

so long to pull out his money
it's as if he's inventing it.

The tiny cashier, also Not-From-Here,
pinches the rub of his soiled bills.

A map of sweat dries into white roads
on the back of his overalls.

Those roads, like many roads here
in the Middle East, lead nowhere.

He receives no change.
He smells like—he's so thin that—

what died inside those overalls?
My wallet bulges with small bills

in this rich, tiny country. Alone here,
like him. But I would die working one

of his 12-hour shifts in 115° heat.
I say that with the certainty

of my passport, for they have not taken
mine. I am buying an exotic fruit

with enormous seeds just to try it.
I do not know its name.

We who are Not-From-Here are cool
and lost, miniature and resigned, speechless

with each other in this enormous mega-store
that sells anything the tiny cashier can scan.

Hope is an invention too. Just ask God.
If you can find him in this long line.

Suppose / *Carolyn Dack Maki*

that Rejoice didn't have an electronic tether slapped on
by immigration agents whose best advice was to get married
to prevent deportation to Nigeria.
Her family's arms are not open to her.

What if
four-year-old son Frederick born out of wedlock wasn't a U.S. citizen.
Nothing about him resembles "anchor baby."
This gregarious child loved by all carries a death sentence.
Mother's indiscretions and Western education are condemned.

And
that Rejoice wasn't admitted to a graduate aviation program
that she didn't have family-supporting employment
that the job anticipated through her high-ranking uncle now comes
with a calling card from Boko Haram's midnight murder squads.

Suppose
that she wasn't trying to abide by U.S. law pleading for asylum.
Now she must report for detention and deportation
rampant under U.S. policy she's dispassionately told.
Tonight she sits with a bottle of Tylenol wondering if this is an answer.

Consider
that tomorrow she might approach a casual acquaintance
with a marriage proposal. Please, she will beg. I'll support you.
Yes, I am using you. You can use me.
So contrary to her Christian faith.

Suppose
that she would be successful in saving their lives,
that her birth name is prophetic.
that their future could mean joy.
Just suppose.

Saint Denis of Migraines, be with us as we lose our way / *Jennifer Clark*

Beheaded in Paris, you continued to preach,
walking six miles before dropping your crown.
Keep us upright as we lumber blindly from bed,

walk on needles in search of medicine.
Like you, we hold our heads in our hands
as the world spins. Where is the path?

Patron Saint of Paris, you are a French ghetto now,
a mosaic of misery and chic stores. Your people
are not considered Parisian enough. In your medieval

heart they thump about, immigrants choked off.
Obstructed, they circulate amongst themselves;
oxygen grows poorer. Mosques and temples throb.

We twitch at the slightest movement.
Eyes squint, squatters steep like tea, dunked
in France's failure to welcome the stranger.

Root cellars—once lined with rampion
and rutabaga, cabbage and kohlrabi—
swell with fear and weapons.

Come, fill our cellars with pork and no pork.
Let veil and no veil rest side by side.
See us through these harsh winters.

Even as we turn away
from our neighbors,
help us yearn for light.

Blue Heron / *Hedy Habra*

An Egyptian sculpture
lost in the Northern wilderness,
the blue heron stands out
in the whitened landscape,
mimics an ibis' fixed stare,
studies the frozen creek,
sensing trembling gills
beneath the transparent sheet.

But why land in my backyard
I wonder, where no lotus ever grows?
Unless he sees his own ancestral roots
in my wide-open eyes lined with kohl,
and knows that water from the Nile
still runs in my veins since birth.

In warmer seasons he has seen me
feed the silver fish,
tend the vegetable garden,
bend over perennials
springing stronger each year,
add more seeds,
making this our home,
where we've lived the longest ever.

Today he saw me walk in circles
in the stillness of barren trees
over crisp snowflakes
masking all signs of life,
the forget-me-nots throbbing
under their icy coat, scintillating,

a thousand suns
opening a dam of flowing memories
of sunnier shores
promises of blossoms to come

until suddenly, as if pulsated by an engine,
statuesque, the migrant bird deploys gigantic
wings, disappears through the dead branches.

ear Iraq,

You
are my
hometown.

I remember
my favorite five-year-old
memories, like when I celebrated
my birthday.

Do you remember
how much I love you?

I love you more than
everything.

Sometimes,
I wonder if you're
doing all right.

Thank you for
the best memories.

Sincerely,

Nada Alhasnawi

A Drive with Mondrian / *Bryan R. Monte*

Rolling down the A2 on my way
home from another retrospective
at Amsterdam's Stedelijk Museum
I wonder why you abandoned
your realistic green and brown farmyards
then your burgundy, yellow and blue
cross-hatched impressionist windmills
or even the bare, bent cubist trees
with angular black and silver branches
for those obsessive black grids
filled with rectangles of white,
blue, yellow and red.

Was it because you had to leave France
during the First World War
that you renounced cubism
and reduced your palette
for your own constructivism?
Was it the flat Dutch fields
bordered by regularly spaced canals
that made you enclose everything
within black grids that became
your style, the signature you took
back to Paris and into a second exile
first to London and then to Manhattan
where you died, a septuagenarian pasting
color cut outs on bare studio walls?

Why so few colors
bounded by black lines?
Was it restful? Did it help
you forget those wild years,
as you waited out the first war?
Was it an attempt to make a name
among *de Stijl's* Dutch artists,
or to find the peace and order you sought
in Blavatsky's or Steiner's societies
or did you just copy Van Doesburg's
stained glass window plan, circa 1918?
I ask myself, strapped into my wheelchair
inside an intercity, disabled cab
travelling 100 kph down the motorway
passing the same five, color cars:
black, white, blue, yellow and red,
rolling down the A2's asphalt lanes.

Even the Sun has its Dark Side / *Hedy Habra*

but does it really matter,
        unless
we could enter that hidden space,
        the way grains of sand
                would suddenly rise
in an hourglass,
        reshape themselves,
        regain their initial place.
I wonder what is lost behind a picture,
        rippled in its negative
as I often try to read between the lines,
        sense clenched teeth,
                or grasp an unspoken word.

When I set to bridge these gaps,
my blood warms up in tides,
        revealing a tightness inside the chest
                as if memories,
        pressed in a tin can
        kept near one's heart,
could sweep away the grayness outside.

We lost everything when we fled,
except for an album
        full of my childhood pictures in Egypt
        and my children born in Beirut.
"You're so lucky," everyone said,
        our family unharmed,
                not one of their fingers
                was worth the whole world
left behind.
        Our beds were made in places
        where the sun teased us, hiding
        most of the time, forcing us to master
        the local motto
                ...make sunshine inside...
Christmases followed one another
        offering versions of our lives,

each fragmented image
evoking a new face,
a recipe ...an absence...

Whenever I sort them out,
I see myself floating in a fluid
lining edges
in search of a referent that has vanished,
leaving only an empty shell,
crumpled, discolored like fallen leaves.

I felt constantly renewed,
peeled off like an onion,
shedding layer after layer
until what was left
was so tender,
une primeur à déguster,
yet so vulnerable.

ear Iraq,

You were my favorite place ever.
I remember how many friends I had there.
Do you remember that I was born there?
Even my family was born there.

I love how the fresh winds blew through my hair.
Sometimes, I wonder why I had to move that fast?
I sometimes miss you so much.

Thank you for being the best friend I ever had.

Your friend,

Taema Qwam-Alden

Guest Workers / *Jim Daniels*

Imported, contracted, indentured stick men,
high in enormous desert sky, guide cranes
with steel chains under gushing heat
of the erupting thermometer someone lied
about to keep men working

and no one claims to be that someone lurking
in the shade of some man-made oasis, shredding
dignity into the bodies of men falling.
Draped in overalls, face-masked against sand,
squiggly flesh lines high in the haze. They bus them in,
bus them out, without tour guide or photo ops.

After they fall, sand scrubs them away
and another stick chalks himself up there
building giant steel insects, antenna lit against night sky
weaving glittered cocoons mirrored against men.

Architects give each other awards in the silence
after completion. Stick men don't stick around.
They wire money back to the Land of Too Poor
to Stick Around, waiting in long lines for the privilege.
Maybe all they want is an afternoon at the shopping mall

but someone has posted signs up against it.
The construction workers are dropping
like flies. But no worries. They were just visiting.

81

An Interview with Gulnar Husain / *Jennifer Clark*

Hospitality can be a radical act, particularly when one steps out of her comfort zone to indiscriminately welcome, accept, and love others. Gulnar Husain marches through her own fears and discomforts to welcome and connect with people from cultures and religions beyond her own.

For almost a decade, Gulnar has cherished her position with Communities In Schools of Kalamazoo (CIS). As the CIS Site Coordinator for Arcadia Elementary School, Gulnar has nurtured a climate of hospitality while surrounding a diverse population of students with whatever it takes—from tutors and food assistance to health services and mentoring—so they can succeed in school, graduate and be prepared for life.

A few years ago, she reached out to First Congregational Church of Kalamazoo. The partnership began with one volunteer, Dianne Roberts, who said she could offer knitting lessons to students. Soon, 48 students were taking time out of their recess to knit baby hats. The students, Gulnar pointed out, were knitting more than yarn. They were forming new friendships and practicing teamwork as she and Dianne had structured the project to span the school's three lunch recesses. Kindergartners worked on hats during their recess and left their work—at whatever point they were at—on the chairs. The next batch of students came in and picked up where the younger students left off. Ultimately, the children wove 500 hats for newborns. I've never seen Gulnar so pleased. *What a beautiful way for our children to welcome the newest members of our community*, she said, clapping her hands.

In the summer of 2016, diagnosed with pancreatic cancer, Gulnar set down her ever-unfinished efforts of knitting community resources into a school. Another pair of hands picked up Gulnar's fine work and continues where she left off.

In December, I went to Gulnar's home to interview her. A dozen boxes and bags were sprinkled throughout the Husain's otherwise pristine home. Gulnar had been collecting a slew of school supplies, clothing, and other basic need items for CIS Kids' Closet. *These snowsuits must get to Arcadia! I know how much the children need them. Oh, and take this bag of magazines to Mr. Aleman, please. He likes to use these with his students. Oh, and....*

Later, her husband, Shagil, a kind and generous man, would help me load my car with the donations she had gathered over the past several months.

When you help a student or family it is such a good feeling, Gulnar has often told me. *I'm always aware and conscious, though, that in many situations, whatever I do is not enough. I help my VISTAs, interns, volunteers, and partners deal with this feeling as it can be frustrating. I remind them, tell them, keep your eyes on what you can do, what you can accomplish.*

Despite her health challenges, Gulnar is still focused on what she can do for others. While cancer may have weakened her physically, Gulnar refuses to allow it to curtail her hospitality. Despite my protests, she slowly walked back and forth from the kitchen to the living room to pour tea and serve me pasties she had made, a delicacy in Pakistan. I stopped fighting her hospitality and snuggled into her couch, ate her warm, buttery pasties, and sipped hot tea.

Gulnar isn't the easiest person to interview. Besides walking in and out of the room, she didn't care to talk about awards she's received over the years, from her 2013 honorable mention for the Unsung Hero Award, given by National Communities In Schools (for doing whatever it takes to eliminate barriers to student success) to her most recent award as the Western Michigan University Department of Political Science 2016 alumna winner of the Timothy Hurttgam Memorial Award. Gulnar did discuss the recent welcoming proclamation made by the City of Kalamazoo. The proclamation declares support for Muslim communities, affirms religious pluralism, and urges Kalamazoo residents to stand together for peace and understanding. She neglected to mention that she is the one who helped to craft it, along with a rabbi, a United Methodist minister, and Kalamazoo's vice mayor.

Ask her a question and she will tell you a story. I'm not complaining. I love Gulnar and am always intrigued to see where her stories take me. Here's a few.

On missing Pakistan

I miss family most of all. My elders are all gone but my cousins are still there. The country itself is enough for me to miss it. I belong to the land. I was raised there. It's where I made best friends, learned from my teachers. I went to a convent school from pre-kindergarten through high school. It was run by Belgian nuns. In the convent school, we weren't allowed to speak any language but English. Even at home. *Speak English around the clock!* they said. Perhaps, as students, we lied and told the teachers we spoke English at home. My mother didn't know any English so she couldn't anyways.

The nuns, they were quite strict. *Speak English around the clock!* We had to wear our clothes a certain length and if it wasn't long enough, they'd send us home. One of their other rules: *no nail polish!* I used to love nail polish! I would put it on at the start of the weekend, and then forget to take off. So I would keep my hands under the desk. With one nail, I would try to scratch the polish off. Oh, I was scared of the sisters! But those were the good old days. We didn't resent our teachers or their rules. Especially as we grew older and appreciated all they taught us. I've stayed in contact with many of the students I went to school with. They all live in Pakistan.

On fate

I was married in July of 1980 in Pakistan. It was arranged. Shaghil and I were classmates in the University. I was not willing to come to America. It's very hard to leave your country. I could never leave my mom and come so far away. But he said he will just be a year or two in America for his studies and then return. That was his plan. We feel we are in control but it is fate that drives us.

My mom, her brothers and sisters were her life blood and she couldn't leave them. She wanted to live in her country and be buried in Pakistan. But whatever is written, is written. My mother, she was here, visiting me in America, when she fell very sick. She went into cardiac arrest and ended up in intensive care. Eventually, we moved her to Canada to be with my sister. She is buried in Canada. We cannot control these things.

On loving America

I arrived in America on January 17th of 1981 in a snowstorm. I landed in Chicago. My husband, along with a big group of his friends, had come to receive me at O'Hare Airport. This was my first time seeing so much snow! That first winter was bad. It was depressing to see white on the ground, on cats and rooftops. Even the sky appeared white. My husband was already attending Western as a graduate student. He had registered me and talked to the chair of the Political Science Department. He had classes during the week and on the weekends, the police warned people to stay put because of the temperatures and mountains of snow.

It was very hard to leave my country but when I came to America, I was so surprised. At service desks, at the bank, everyone was so welcoming. Because I was enrolled in school at Western, I had health insurance through the university's health center. The receptionist there was so nice and helpful. And now, when I go to the Cancer Center, the nurses, they go out of their way and are so polite and helpful. This American sense of service and taking care of others, it's very noticeable.

I have appreciated everything about America but what I appreciate the most is the concept of service. Here in America is this idea of serving others and being fair in your dealings. You do not see this in Pakistan. I have felt so welcome and that is part of why I stayed.

On sacred music

My daughter, Sarah, was born in 1984. Because of her, I started volunteering. But it was after 2001, after 9/11, when the Kalamazoo Islamic Center began receiving many interfaith requests that I became involved with so many groups my husband said, *You are never home in the evenings anymore.* But he never asked me to stop, so I continued.

It is quite surprising that I became involved in the Michigan Festival of Sacred Music as there is zero music in Islam. In mosques and religious services there is chanting but no music. I never learned music and so I have no temperament for music. My sister loved listening to music on BBC. It was mostly American and British music. I only have an ear from her. So when I was asked to do this I said, *I have no interest in music. I'm not the right person. There is no sacred music in Islam.*

At the time, Dr. Mushtaq Luqmani, chair of the board of Kalamazoo Islamic Center at that time, continued to push. You think I am persistent! He is even more so. *There must be something we can do,* he kept saying. *Perhaps our young children can sing?* So Sarah found a few songs for me. One was Tala' al-Badru 'Alaynā. The children learned the lyrics and sang it in

Arabic. Muhammed was born in Mecca and he, along with a group of his followers, later migrated to Medina. In Medina, people who were not family and did not know the Prophet, welcomed him. When Muhammed reached Medina, the children came out of their homes and sang:

> *Oh, the white moon rose over us*
> *From the valley of Wadia*
> *And we owe it to show gratefulness*
> *where the call is to Allah*
> *Oh you who were raised among us*
> *Coming with a word to be obeyed*
> *You have brought to this city nobleness*
> *Welcome best caller to God's way*

As the children went around singing this song and others, people said, *How do we introduce you?* They wanted a name. *You must have a name,* they said. My friends and family said, *Call it the Muslim Youth Choir* and so that's what we called it. And then the children were singing everywhere. People would come to me and ask, *Do you do this professionally? Would you come to our town? Can you bring your choir to our city and sing for us?* How ashamed I felt, them asking me. For years we did this. There was no instrumental music with it, though, so it was okay.

On Islam and immigration

This is the history, the spread of Islam: immigrants being welcomed by these little children of Medina. In that time, the people who emigrated with the Prophet Muhammed, they were called Mujahir. And those people that helped to settle the immigrants were called Ansar.

Prophet was very particular about how we should treat others. He said to them both, they are your brothers and you are their brothers and you do not differentiate between them. Much like Jesus, yes, when he said, "*Who is my brother?*"

Yes, we are all brothers and sisters. We are of the same chain.

On learning a lesson while teaching a lesson

America is a welcoming country. Everyone is welcome here, I once told a group of students at King-Westwood Elementary School. I was an AmeriCorps worker then with Communities In Schools and giving a talk on Pakistan.

There was this male teacher—Mr. Miller, a fifth grade teacher, who is, I believe, still teaching there. Oh, I was so impressed by him. I still think of that moment. I was talking of America being a melting pot, and he stopped me, interrupted me and said, *It's not a melting pot!* With a melting pot, he explained, individuals lose their identity. He went on to say that if you are cooking a dish and add five vegetables, those vegetables form a new flavor. Qualities of those individual ingredients do not retain their original flavor. They lose their individual properties. *In America*, he said, *we cherish everyone's own identities and accept them as they are.*

I thought about that later and I never used the world 'melting pot' after that.

On public speaking

After 9/11, the Islamic Center had been receiving many invitations from churches to speak and we had to arrange something. It was either go out and face the crowd or say no. I felt that responsibility. This is a need our community had—I don't mean just the Pakistani or immigrant community, but all of Kalamazoo. All sides needed this. We were living in our own cubicles and people wanted to know us. I owed it to all sides. *I must do this and get through this*, I said to myself.

The first time I spoke was at a huge church, a cathedral, off of Oakland Drive. I had written down what I was going to say. I rehearsed what I'd written many times. I was so nervous. When I got there, I realized it was a circular hall and the stage was in the middle, the crowd all around you. I saw it and panicked. I told the pastor of the church, *I am going to run out!* and she said, *No, we are going to lock these doors now.* Ha! Well, I managed to stay there. Those doors were so big. Oh, those walls were so tall! I heard my voice, the words came to me and I spoke. *You did not seem nervous at all*, people later told me. I don't know how that was possible as I was nervous to the end. I have given many talks since then, but I'm always nervous when I speak.

87

On the shift

I hold America in the highest regard. But lately, things are changing and this is concerning. America has always been service-oriented and valued the importance of looking after its neighbors. But after 2001, that seems to be slowly diminishing. And you notice it. It is for no other reason than you look different. In our town, we have one mall. We shop at the same places we have shopped at for the past 35 or 36 years and now the service people are not as polite. Some are very rude. Not too often, but yes, it happens.

On what we must do

We must work harder, uniting, and working together to combat the xenophobia. We are fortunate that we have so much going on in our little town to combat this fear. At a Kalamazoo City Commission meeting in March 2016, a proclamation was announced. Let me see, I have a copy of it. Here it is! See here, this is the "Proclamation: Welcoming and Respectful Community." We are a city that welcomes refugees. And I just learned that at Arcadia School, the teachers are learning Arabic. That is the America I came to!

I am very encouraged by all the help and support that is being done. By this local community, especially in Kalamazoo. People are speaking out to say this is not who we are, but rather, this is what America is and should be. This must continue. I hope, sooner than later, the voice of the better ones will prevail.

On the Level / *Bryan R. Monte*

I struggle to stay upright on the platform
leaning against the side of the train
at Utrecht station, pushed and jostled
from behind as I swing my rig up two steps
while no one offers assistance.
Passengers stream and squeeze past
then sit down in the disabled chairs
next to the entrance, suddenly blind
or staring off into space as I roll up,
seemingly unaware of the pictograms
of canes and wheelchairs printed
into the upholstery under their bottoms
or on the blue and white signs
posted on the wall above their heads
until I say: *Goede morgen, middag* or *avond*
and ask for a volunteer to yield a seat
their blunt, blank stares turning to icy daggers.

At "America's most unfriendly city's"[1] airport
the wheelchair attendants argue
over who is going to push "Him!"
to and through security as if I were deaf
and not sitting just a few feet away.
The loser starts pushing me slowly
to the wrong end of the terminal
even though I protest,
so I don't miss my flight,
my comfort in the hands of a hostile stranger.
I think "No tip" and thank God
for those thin pieces of plastic
in my wallet and the meet and greet
driver numbers programmed in my cell phone
(if I do miss a flight and need to stay the night)
since now I must roll everywhere I go
just to keep things on the level.

---

[1] Rated in edition.cnn.com/2014/08/06/travel/us-unfriendliest-friendliest-cities/

**Dear Mexico,**

You are my home. You are the place
I should be at right now.
I remember being there and me, dad, mom, sister,
and brother went on a walk and to the store.
Do you remember me and my family?
We miss you a lot. Do you remember
that my brother was born there?
I love your plants and flowers and the grass.
There was no snow.
I love you, Mexico.
I miss you. I wonder
if you are growing plants,
if you have lot of shops.
I miss you a lot. I love you.
I wish I was there right now.
You are my home.

Thank you for being there for me
when I was over there.

Lizbet Lopez

Creamed Corn / *Ted Kooser*

The Jamaicans who came to can corn
at the Green Giant plant in the '40s
were sinuously thin and so black
that a lame word offered to them in greeting
went right through their skins without
raising a ripple. Our own black families
(we spoke that way, of 'our' black families),
the Martins and Shipps, had lived among us
so long it no longer mattered,
but these Jamaicans were different.
They kept to themselves, in loose clusters,
and knives flashed from the shadows
when they picked their teeth or scraped
Iowa from under their pale, perfect nails.
And when they talked they sounded like pianos;
all over the keyboard went their honky-tonk
laughing and talking. Word got around
that out of pure spite and meanness
sometimes they peed in the creamed corn
as it sluffed through the trough. Then the plant
shut down for the year, and they were gone,
and neighborly old Bob Martin rose up
and went down, up and down, in his place,
running the lift in our only hotel. Years later,
wherever we've gone, whatever we've come to,
our ignorance spoils the creamed corn.

Pantoum of Ignorance / *Carolyn Dack Maki*

War starts on Aisle 6
When a Muslim woman dresses as tradition requires
Meets two little brothers wearing camo.
Confrontation begins between Old El Paso and Prego

When a Muslim woman dresses as tradition requires.
Sarah shudders as finger Uzis kill her.
Confrontation begins between Old El Paso and Prego.
The mother laughs at her sons' combative readiness.

Sarah shudders as finger Uzis kill her.
The hijab cannot hide the horror shot through her body.
The mother laughs at her sons' combative readiness
As Egyptian husband steps in to save wife's dignity.

The hijab cannot hide the horror shot through her body.
Once smiling eyes now have tears
As Egyptian husband steps in to save wife's dignity.
See the lifted veil and lips saying, "Hi, I am Sarah."

Once smiling eyes now have tears.
Meets two little brothers wearing camo.
See the lifted veil and lips saying, "Hi, I am Sarah."
War starts on Aisle 6.

Every year, the corpses of hundreds of immigrants are flown from
San Francisco to their home countries.

San Francisco Weekly,
Lauren Smiley, January 20, 2009

Exporting the Dead / *Jennifer Clark*

When an elephant dies
bones rest and relatives remember;
wrinkled trunks inhale the scent of skull,
then silently caress ivory tusks.
Massive feet rise, and soft
as a whisper, stroke that which remains.

When a human—deemed illegal—dies
the good death begins; it is in
the business of 'international transfers'
that a life no longer, is legitimized.
Documents once withheld
made up for now, an offering
of papers—presented to the corpse—
certified and sealed, pinned to
that which remains, like a
note from a guilty parent:
we withhold love no longer.

It costs more to fly dead
than alive, even though the dead
don't ask for pillows.
In this sport of exporting
we pretend they're alive.

So when a human dies illegal
bones fly home
or glide on the backs of waves
to Mexico, Nicaragua, El Salvador
for singing relatives to bury.
A mother folds her arms and hugs herself.
A sea of feet stand above blanketed bones
and remember that their dead once lived.

A Glimpse of Fall / *Hedy Habra*

My art teacher says,
"Never paint a tree
in spring or summer,
paint them nude,
when you can see them
embrace each other,
when their antlered arms
raise in different directions."

It's too cold to paint
outdoors where the river
begins to melt under
ducks' emerald green.

I'm glad the next-door
neighbors didn't build.
Their tall crackled oaks
will be mine a while longer
still covered with
shriveled sandy-ochre leaves.

Leaves dry, cling
to their old birthplace.
I think of my mother
who always wanted
to be buried in Egypt
beside her husband, mother,
in their family vault.
Now, she'll be buried
in the New World.

When I'd tell her,
"I'm taller than you
now," she'd say,
"Don't you know people
shrink with age? I wasn't
always like this."

I try to pull the crisp
auburn leaves, one by one.
They look old, dead,
but alive inside.
They won't give up
until a new leaf
pushes them aside.

ear Syria,

You make me feel happy.
I remember the sound of the ocean in Tartas.
Do you remember when we were grilling on your beach?
I love your amusement parks.
Sometimes, I wonder what you will be like when I return to you in fifteen years?
Thank you for giving me happiness.

Your daughter,

Hala Alhasan

World Religions / *Jim Daniels*
upon returning to Pittsburgh

The Koran and the Bible together on a shelf now,
below and to the right of the travel books
and above the children's books we've outgrown
but cannot part with.

I like to think they are comparing notes
on Abraham and Jesus
and other common kin
as they gather dust
until it is visible.

Kinship and Kindness / *Scott Russell Sanders*

[Editors' note: John Woolman was an 18th century Quaker and abolitionist. Earlier in the essay (this is an excerpt), the author notes that "Woolman believed that each person carries an "inner light," representing the presence of God within and offering guidance in the conduct of life."]

We stand in sore need of broad fellow-feeling today, as environmental devastation makes life more difficult not only for the poor and the outcast, and not only for humans, but for all creatures. So it would be valuable to know what gives rise to this impulse, and how we might foster it, in ourselves and in our society. If one does not share Woolman's belief in the inner light, with its promptings from God, how else to account for the extraordinary range of his sympathies?

Evolutionary psychologists might interpret this all-inclusive sympathy as an expression of the capacity for social bonding inherent in all of us, but which is carried to an extreme in a Woolman or Gandhi or Mandela, just as our capacity for reasoning flowers spectacularly in a Newton or Einstein. The premise of evolutionary psychology is that the brain, like the rest of the body, inherits structures favoring reproductive success, physiological adaptations winnowed by natural selection and sexual selection. In the case of the brain, these structures are neural patterns, such as the fear reflex triggered by the sight of a spider or snake, or the desire stirred by signs of biological fitness in a potential mate, or the nurturing instinct elicited by the sight of a newborn. This theory can account for fellow-feeling toward one's genetic kin, where the reproductive advantages are clear; it can also account for altruism shown toward non-kin who share physical features or cultural practices with one's blood relations. More broadly, the theory explains the adaptive benefit of solidarity with one's tribe, since a tightly bonded group is more likely to defend its members from predators and rival groups— hence our propensity for dividing the world between insiders and outsiders.

But what might expand the sense of solidarity beyond the circumference of kinfolk and tribe, even beyond our own species? How to explain the comprehensive and often hazardous sympathy shown by John Woolman or Martin Luther King, Jr. and a host of others, from venerated figures such as the Buddha and Jesus to the unheralded peacemakers and caretakers in every community and every age? As a follower of Jesus, Woolman took seriously the instruction to love his neighbor as he would love his own children, without placing any restriction on who that neighbor might be, since all were children of God. Followers of the Buddha take seriously the vow to relieve the suffering of all sentient beings, no matter how impossible the task. More recently, conservationists have espoused an ethic, most cogently articulated by Aldo Leopold, that expands the boundaries of caring to include the lands and waters and atmosphere and the whole community of life.

That we so often fail to live up to these ideals can be taken as evidence of our selfishness and clannishness; less clear, from an evolutionary perspective, is what might give rise to such calls for universal benevolence in the first place. The Buddha lived to a ripe old age, but produced no offspring; Jesus was executed, and likewise left no offspring; Gandhi and King were assassinated; Leopold died of a heart attack while fighting a wildfire on a neighbor's land; Woolman could easily have perished on his journey or been murdered by slaveholders. Every day's news brings stories about doctors, aid workers, and volunteers risking and often losing their lives in efforts to help strangers suffering from war, disease, and natural disasters. What force could override the selfish demands of the gene and the boundaries of the tribe?

Without discounting what can be learned from evolutionary psychology, I think a deeper answer may be found by consulting ecology and physics.

Suppose, for example, you are studying a frog native to the Amazon rainforest. You learn that phosphorus, a nutrient vital to plant growth, leaches steadily out of the Amazon due to heavy rainfall and flooding, so you wonder how the forest continues to thrive. You discover that a fresh supply of phosphorus is delivered each year by dust carried across the Atlantic Ocean on massive storms originating in the Sahara desert. Much of that dust comes from a dried-up lakebed in Chad, where the sediment contains the phosphorus-rich remains of diatoms that once lived in freshwater lakes. Meanwhile, the nutrients washing down the Amazon River into the Atlantic support vast blooms of phytoplankton, which in turn supports all levels of marine life, from krill to humpback whales. At present, this nourishing cycle works marvelously well. However, the amount of dust wafted from Africa depends on the amount of rainfall in the Sahara, and that amount will change, in unpredictable ways, as the climate warms. Heavier rain in the desert will mean less phosphorus in the rainforest. So the fate of your frog and its home in the Amazon basin, the most biodiverse habitat on Earth, is ultimately linked to the burning of coal in Indiana power plants, the gushing of methane from cattle feedlots in Argentina, the idling of cars at stoplights in cities, the hustling of diesel trucks on the world's highways, the thawing of tundra in the Artic, and every other source of greenhouse gases.

What ecology has revealed is that all of Earth's varied habitats, species, and organisms are bound up in an integral whole. The physician and essayist Lewis Thomas memorably compared our planet's interconnectedness with that of a living cell. As in a cell, Earth is surrounded by a protective membrane—the geomagnetic field and atmosphere that deflect the solar wind and absorb ultraviolet radiation, while admitting sunlight and insulating our planet from the deep freeze of space. Within that membrane, there is a constant exchange of energy and materials. Humans are part of that flow; it makes us and sustains us. We might think of ourselves as autonomous, but every molecule of air we breathe has passed through other lungs and through the pores of leaves. Every atom in our bodies has passed through other bodies, through flowers and ferns, through rivers and rocks. After we die, those atoms will keep circulating. There are no fixed points, no hard edges. Every seeming boundary, from the skin enveloping one's body to the borders between nations, is permeable, temporary, ever shifting. The flow never ceases.

State of Michigan, United States of America

Proclamation

Welcoming and Respectful Community

WHEREAS, the City of Kalamazoo has long been recognized as a hospitable and welcoming community, where people, families, and institutions thrive, and the contributions of all are celebrated and valued. Residents of the City of Kalamazoo live up to our highest American values of acceptance and equality, and treat newcomers with decency and respect, creating a vibrant community for all to live in; and,

WHEREAS, the City of Kalamazoo has long been home to immigrants from around the world, who come seeking opportunity, stability, prosperity, and a better life for their families. The City of Kalamazoo is home to immigrants who come from regions such as the Middle East, Latin America, Africa, Europe, and Asia. The city's diverse communities consist of first and second generation immigrants as well as African-Americans who have historically migrated from the southern United States; and,

WHEREAS, the Welcoming Kalamazoo Initiative aims to build cooperation, respect, and compassion among all in our community, including immigrants and non-immigrants alike; endeavors to create a more inclusive society, and seeks to embrace cultural, religious and ethnic diversity; and,

WHEREAS, the City of Kalamazoo community remembers, honors, and values our immigrant and migrant roots, and embraces the values of family, faith, and hard work; and,

WHEREAS, our city has greatly benefited from the addition of community members from all religious backgrounds, including those who have moved here in the past, who have become valued citizens, significantly contributing to the betterment of our community; and,

WHEREAS, our Muslim community, both native born and immigrant, is an integral part of Kalamazoo's diversity, plurality, and of our growing multicultural identity, representing an increasingly important thread in the tapestry of American society; and,

WHEREAS, Muslims, inspired by their faith, give back every day as U.S. military personnel, police officers, doctors, nurses, caregivers, teachers, clergy, and in many other roles, contributing to the success of the United States of America and the City of Kalamazoo; and,

WHEREAS, there has been an increase in anti-Muslim and anti-immigration rhetoric among politicians and in the national media, with an increase of hate speech and violence targeting Muslim families and children across our nation, which is detrimental to all people who cherish safety, freedom and liberty; and

102

WHEREAS, such stereotyping and fear-mongering only leads to alienation and vicious, even deadly, acts of intolerance; and

WHEREAS, The City of Kalamazoo finds this anti-Muslim rhetoric and hate violence to be against American values of religious freedom and fairness and contrary to the vision we hold as a nation that welcomes all people; and

WHEREAS, Kalamazoo is a city that does not tolerate hate speech or hate crimes and all of Kalamazoo's residents deserve to live in a safe environment free of hate and discrimination; and,

WHEREAS, recent demands seeking a ban on Muslims entering this country are unconscionable, and if carried forward, would constitute violations of the 1st and 14th Amendments to the U.S. Constitution, which is tragically reminiscent of prior historic racial and religious profiling; and,

WHEREAS, this country was founded on principles of plurality, freedom of religion, and freedom from religious persecution; and,

WHEREAS, the City of Kalamazoo wishes to extend the traditional Islamic greeting of "Peace be upon you" to all of its Muslim residents and visitors.

NOW, THEREFORE, BE IT RESOLVED, Kalamazoo and its City Commissioners stand in support of our Muslim community, and call for an end to the continued use of anti-Muslim and anti-immigration hate speech; and,

BE IT FURTHER RESOLVED, Kalamazoo will continue to be a welcoming city to Muslims from all over the world, including immigrants and those fleeing from violence, persecution and injustice; and,

BE IT FURTHER RESOLVED, that the City of Kalamazoo is affirmed as a place where all foreign-born and native-born Americans can live, work, and play together; share in each other's customs and ideals, and appreciate and promote cultural diversity. We urge residents and stakeholders of the Kalamazoo community to join with the efforts and spirit of the Welcoming Michigan Initiative and others to join in lifting up the City of Kalamazoo as a welcoming environment for all.

Bobby J. Hopewell,
Mayor

103

The New Colossus

[Editor's note: This sonnet was written in 1883 by Emma Lazarus. It is engraved on a bronze plaque and mounted on the pedestal on which the Statue of Liberty stands.]

Not like the brazen giant of Greek fame,
With conquering limbs astride from land to land;
Here at our sea-washed, sunset gates shall stand
A mighty woman with a torch, whose flame
Is the imprisoned lightning, and her name
Mother of Exiles. From her beacon-hand
Glows world-wide welcome, her mild eyes command
The air-bridged harbor that twin cities frame.

"Keep ancient lands, your storied pomp!" cries she
With silent lips. "Give me your tired, your poor,
Your huddled masses yearning to breathe free,
The wretched refuse of your teeming shore.
Send these, the homeless, tempest-tost to me,
I lift my lamp beside the golden door!"

Acknowledgements

The "Dear Country," letters as well as the group poem that appear in this anthology were created during two "lunch & learn" poetry workshops held at Arcadia Elementary School. Special thanks to Arcadia Elementary School, Communities In Schools of Kalamazoo, Kalamazoo Public Schools, and the following individuals for helping to lift the voices of our youth: Donia Ali, Caitlin Bale, Nicholas Baxter, Grace Gheen, Cindy Hadley, and Greg Socha.

Thanks to Kalamazoo Public Schools teachers Debora Gant, Holly Bishop, Erin Young, and Donna Judd for the opportunity to work with such wonderful students.

Thanks to Elizabeth Kerlikowske for her guidance and support throughout the making of this anthology.

We are grateful to Friends of Poetry, Inc. for their support with this project.

A special thanks to all Justice For Our Neighbor (JFON) volunteers and immigration lawyers throughout the entire JFON network who work tirelessly to welcome and support immigrants.

All pieces within the anthology are the copyright of their authors. We thank them all for lending their voice to this important project. We also thank the following publishers and journals where some of the poems and essays in this anthology were first published:

Teresa Mei Chuc: "Immigration" first appeared in the chapbook *Cartesian Product*, Silkworms Ink, 2010. "Quan Âm on a Dragon" first appeared in *Whitefish Review*, 2015. "Family" first appeared in *Masque & Spectacle Magazine*, 2015.

Jennifer Clark: "Exporting the Dead" first published in *Complex Allegiances*, Universal Table/Wising Up Press. From *Necessary Clearings* (Shabda Press, 2014).

Hedy Habra: "Blue Heron" first published in the anthology Come Together: Imagine Peace (2008). "The Bullfrog" first published by *Black Buzzard Review*. "A Glimpse of Fall" first published by *Negative Capability*. "Even the Sun has its Dark Side" first published by *Inclined to Speak: An Anthology of Contemporary Arab American Poetry* (2008). All four poems are from *Tea in Heliopolis* (Press 53, 2013).

Ted Kooser: "Creamed Corn" first appeared in *Delights & Shadows*, Copper Canyon Press (2004).

Carolyn Dack Maki: "Suppose" first published in *New Verse News*.

Jack Ridl: "Ridl Was Once Spelled Hridl" and "Hands" first published in *Practicing to Walk Like a Heron* (Wayne State University Press, 2013).

John Rybicki: "Traveling at High Speeds" first published in *The Quarterly*. From *Traveling at High Speeds* (New Issues Press, 2003).

Scott Russell Sanders: These two excerpts are from "They're Neighbors of Mine" © 2015 by Scott Russell Sanders; first published in *Notre Dame Magazine*; and "Kinship and Kindness" © 2016; first published in *Orion*.

Biographical Notes

Kathryn Almy is a freelance writer and an aide at the Kalamazoo Public Library. Her poems and essays have appeared in several print and on-line publications including *City of the Big Shoulders: A Chicago Poetry Anthology, Silver Birch Press,* and *Great Lakes Review's* narrative map.

Nicholas Baxter is a genuine soul, meek and curious about the world and the people within it. After being a musician for half his life, a surgery on his left hand took away this ability. To compensate creatively, he began writing stories about his experiences with people and life.

Marion Boyer is author of two poetry chapbooks and *The Clock of the Long Now,* a poetry book published by Mayapple Press. Born Canadian, at thirteen Boyer became an American citizen and still recalls the strangeness of being called an *alien* who needed to be *naturalized.*

Bonnie Jo Campbell is the bestselling author of *Mothers, Tell Your Daughters* (W.W. Norton), *Once Upon a River,* and *American Salvage,* among other works. She was a National Book Award finalist, NBCC Award finalist, and a Guggenheim Fellow, and the *Guardian* named her one of the top writers of rural noir fiction. She rides a variety of bicycles and donkeys around Kalamazoo, Michigan.

Teresa Mei Chuc, author of two collections of poetry, *Red Thread* (Fithian Press) and *Keeper of the Winds* (FootHills Publishing), was born in Saigon, Vietnam and immigrated to the U.S. under political asylum with her mother and brother shortly after the Vietnam War while her father remained in a Vietcong "reeducation" camp for nine years. Her new chapbook of poetry is *How One Loses Notes and Sounds* (Word Palace Press).

Jennifer Clark is the author of the full-length poetry collection, *Necessary Clearings* (Shabda Press). Her second poetry collection, *Johnny Appleseed: The Slice and Times of John Chapman,* is forthcoming from Shabda Press. Her work has been published in *Columbia Journal, Concho River Review, Flyway, Nimrod,* and *Ecotone,* among other places. She lives in Kalamazoo, Michigan.

Mollie Clements was born in Galveston, Texas. After marrying Jesse Clements in Stockholm, Sweden, they proceeded to the Philippine Islands for a six-month Methodist work camp. They raised four children in Hong Kong, where they worked with refugees for ten years, and then Bombay, where they worked with slum dwellers for four years. Illness sent them back to the U.S. in 1978. Mollie was ordained an elder in the United Methodist Church in 1987, ministered in the outskirts of Chicago, then in an inner city parish in Indianapolis. Following retirement, they moved to Kalamazoo in 2003.

Mollie served as one of the founding co-chairs of First United Methodist of Kalamazoo's Justice Team from 2008 to 2013. Through the Michigan Organizing Project, now Michigan United, she has been on the immigration task force for the past ten years, working on immigration reform and advocacy.

Jim Daniels' next books of poems, *Rowing Inland*, Wayne State University Press, and *Street Calligraphy*, Steel Toe Books, will both be published in 2017. A native of Detroit, Daniels is the Thomas Stockham University Professor of English at Carnegie Mellon University.

Hedy Habra has authored two poetry collections, *Tea in Heliopolis* and *Under Brushstrokes*. Her story collection, *Flying Carpets*, won the 2013 Arab American National Book Award's Honorable Mention. Her poetry appears in *Cimarron Review, Bitter Oleander, Gargoyle, Poet Lore, Nimrod, World Literature Today* and *Verse Daily*. Her website is Hedyhabra.com.

Buddy Hannah is a retired radio talk show host. He is also a playwright, director, and poet. Buddy has performed poetry readings and conducted creative writing workshops throughout Southwest Michigan. Among his many awards are the Irving S. Gilmore Community Medal of Arts Awards and the Tony Griffin Golden Word Award.

Elizabeth Kerlikowkse is president of Friends of Poetry, a non-profit dedicated to bringing people and poetry together. Her most recent book is *Chain of Lakes* from Kalamazoo Book Arts.

Carrie Knowlton is a Public Health Nurse. Born and raised in Kalamazoo, she recently moved back after 20+ years of trying to figure out where home is, exactly.

Ted Kooser served two terms as U. S. Poet Laureate and is a past winner of the Pulitzer Prize in Poetry. His most recent collection of poems is *Splitting an Order*, from Copper Canyon Press, 2014. His fourth children's book, *Mr. Posey's New Glasses,* is forthcoming from Candlewick Press.

Carolyn Dack Maki, retired from Kalamazoo Public Schools and Western Michigan Department of Speech/Language Pathology, has a longtime interest in conflict resolutions. As a founding board member of Springfield Peace School she helped teach conflict resolution strategies. As an accent reduction specialist Carolyn helped English-as-a-Second-Language students enhance communication skills.

Bryan R. Monte is a social anthropologist, writer and editor. Recently his work has appeared in *Assaracus, Friends Journal* (poem and interview at www.youtube.com/watch?v=bPMOKG_nI2E), the *John Whitmer Historical Association Journal*, in the anthology *Gathered: Contemporary Quaker Poets*, and in the online magazines *Poetry Pacific* and the *South Florida Poetry Journal.*

Naomi Shihab Nye is the author or editor of around 35 books, most recently *Famous*, illustrated by Lisa Desimini (Wings Press) and *The Turtle of Oman* (Greenwillow), which won the Middle East Book Award. She is a longtime fan of Kalamazoo and thinks the Promise program is the best thing happening in the United States of America.

Michigan poet, **Lynn Pattison**'s work has appeared in *The Notre Dame Review*, *Rhino, Atlanta Review, Harpur Palate, Smartish Pace, Rattle, Tinderbox, Slipstream,* and *Poetry East*, among others, and been anthologized in several venues. Nominated twice for a Pushcart Prize, she is the author of three collections: *tesla's daughter* (March St. Press); *Walking Back the Cat* (Bright Hill Press) and *Light That Sounds Like Breaking* (Mayapple Press).

Kathy Rabbers grew up on a lake near Three Rivers. College at Michigan State University, library school at Western Michigan University, then left Michigan for Seattle and New York City, an unpredicted bicoastal arrangement that worked great for 30 years. In 2006, she moved back to Michigan, built a house and began to settle. Settling, to her, means a home base, much loved fields nearby, enough travel and then joyfully returning home.

Jack Ridl's *Practicing to Walk Like a Heron* (Wayne State University Press), received the Foreword Reviews Gold Medal for Poetry. His other award winning collections are *Broken Symmetry* (WSUPress), Society of Midland Authors Best Book of Poetry, and *Losing Season* (CavanKerry Press). The Poetry Society of Michigan named him Honorary Chancellor, only the second poet so-named. He is co-author with Peter Schakel of *Approaching Literature* (Bedford/St. Martin's Press). Jack was named by the Carnegie Foundation as Michigan's Professor of the year. More than 85 of his students are now publishing.

John Rybicki's latest book of poems, *When All the World is Old*, is available at Lookout Books. He is also the author of two other collections, *We Bed Down into Water*, and *Traveling at High Speeds*. His prose and poetry have appeared in *Ploughshares, The American Poetry Review, Poetry, Field, TriQuarterly, Ecotone*, and in *The Best American Poetry* and *Pushcart Prize* anthologies. He teaches poetry writing in Detroit schools through the InsideOut Literary Arts Project.

Scott Russell Sanders is the author of 20 books of fiction and nonfiction, including, most recently, *Divine Animal: A Novel* and *Dancing in Dreamtime: Stories*. He is a distinguished professor emeritus of English at Indiana University, in Bloomington, where he and his wife, Ruth, a biochemist, reared their two children.

Phillip Sterling's new book of poetry, *And Then Snow*, will be released in April 2017 from Main Street Rag Press. He is also the author of *In Which Brief Stories Are Told* (fiction), *Mutual Shores* (poetry) and four chapbook-length series of poems: *Significant Others*, *Quatrains*, *Abeyance*, *And for All This: Poems from Isle Royale*. The recipient of a National Endowment for the Arts Fellowship, two Fulbright Awards (Belgium and Poland), a PEN Syndicated Fiction Award, and multiple Pushcart Prize nominations (in poetry and prose), he has served as Artist-in-Residence for both Isle Royale National Park and Sleeping Bear Dunes National Lakeshore.

Lisa Stucky has called Portage home for 28 of the last 29 years. She is an elementary music teacher in Portage Public Schools and uses songs to try to make all children feel welcome, included, and affirmed.

Alison Swan's poems and prose have appeared in many publications, including her books *Before the Snow Moon* and *Dog Heart*, the recent anthologies *The Michigan Poet*, *Here: Women Writing on the Upper Peninsula*, and *Poetry in Michigan/Michigan in Poetry*. Her book *Fresh Water: Women Writing on the Great Lakes* is a Michigan Notable Book. She's been awarded a Mesa Refuge Fellowship and the Michigan Environmental Council's Petoskey Prize for Grassroots Environmental Leadership. She teaches at Western Michigan University and lives in Ann Arbor.

Ritika Verma is a fifth grader at Arcadia Elementary School in Kalamazoo, Michigan and is the daughter of Indian-American immigrants. This is her first publication.

Kelly Zajac owns and operates Tudor House Tea & Spice in Kalamazoo, Michigan, a store that is as much about the welcoming and calming atmosphere as the quality of products offered. A former elementary teacher, she incorporates education into all of her endeavors. Currently, you can find her helping people learn about teas, spices, cooking, and simplifying their lives.

Justice For Our Neighbors

If you could help someone escape persecution or violence, would you? If you could keep a family from being torn apart, would you? If your neighbor needed you, would you be there for them? Immigrants—our newest and often most vulnerable neighbors—need your support. By making a financial contribution to JFON Kalamazoo or any JFON clinic, you do all this and more.

It takes $63,355 a year to run Kalamazoo's JFON clinic. We can't do this work without you. Donate today. Be that voice and helping hand that welcomes and lifts up our newest neighbors.

Your gift can be mailed to:

Justice For Our Neighbors-Kalamazoo
212 S. Park
Kalamazoo, MI 49007

Questions? Call JFON Kalamazoo at (888) 718.7775 or email: kzoo_assist@jfonwestmichigan.org.

JFON Sites Throughout West Michigan

West Michigan Site Headquarters
Phone: (616) 301.7461 Address: 207 Fulton St E, Grand Rapids, Michigan 49503

Holland Satellite
Phone: (616) 396.5595 Address: 57 West 10th, Holland, Michigan 49423

Kalamazoo Satellite
Phone: (888) 718.7775 Address: 212 S. Park, Kalamazoo, MI 49007

Traverse City Satellite
Phone: (231) 620.1100 Address: 222 Cass St, Traverse City, Michigan 49684

www: http://jfonwestmichigan.org/

As of April 2017, there are 35 JFON clinic sites operating nationwide. To see the JFON clinic locations by state, visit the National JFON website and map of clinics by going to: http://njfon.org/our-services/legal-clinics/.